CALLED TO THE CLASSROOM:
Daily Reflections for Educators

Christina Meline

Team Meline
www.teammeline.com

ISBN: 979-8-9881434-0-6

DEDICATION

To all who are doing the impactful, heartbreaking, and rewarding work of raising up our future generations.

You are seen, valued, and known. You are not alone.

CONTENTS

Part 1: I Am Called

Part 2: I Am Connected

Part 3: I Am Courageous

Part 4: I Am Compassionate

Part 5: I Am Creative

Day 121: I Am Creative

Day 122: I Am a Dreamer

Day 123: I Am a Visionary

Day 124: I Am Imaginative

Day 125: I Am a Risk-Taker

Day 126: I Am Inspired

Day 127: I Am Bold

Day 128: I Am Wandering

Day 129: I Am Authentic

Day 130: I Am Simple

Day 131: I Am Complex

Day 132: I Am Unique

Day 133: I Am a Learner

Day 134: I Am Vibrant

Day 135: I Am Observant

Day 136: I Am an Awakener

Day 137: I Am a Motivator

Day 138: I Am Adaptive

Day 139: I Am Lighthearted

Day 140: I Am Gifted

Day 141: I Am Versatile

Day 142: I Am an Artist

Day 143: I Am a Speaker

Day 144: I Am a Writer

Day 145: I Am Playful

Day 146: I Am a Performer

Day 147: I Am Innovative

Day 148: I Am Determined

Day 149: I Am Changing

Day 150: I Am Transformed

Part 6: I Am Celebrated

INTRODUCTION: OUR JOURNEY
A Note from the Author

Dear Reader,

In the wide array of joys and challenges we face in raising up the future generations, faith and connection are foundational. If you're reading this, I imagine you have been called to minister to children and young adults in some capacity. This devotional text is designed to create space for reflection; to pause and center ourselves in our identity in Jesus Christ and remember that we are a part of a community of educators with gritty faith and passionate souls!

Even though I may not know you personally, I feel connected to you through our shared faith and calling. As I wrote these reflections, I imagined sitting next to you, the reader, with a cup of coffee or tea; perhaps with papers waiting to be graded, scattered on the table in front of us. Whether you are a teacher, paraprofessional, administrator, or in another role working with our young people, I pictured us just talking about our day. It is my intention to journey with you in spirit this year. I want to celebrate with you on the days when you're bursting with excitement because of that lesson you've invested so much time and energy into creating! I want to sit and hold your hand on the days when tears fill your eyes before the school day has even started.

I have included 180 devotional reflections in this book, outlined to provide a reading for every school day of your year. Each reflection begins with an identifying word. These words encompass *some* of the many capacities we fill while also reminding us of the identifying truths God speaks over us. My writing style is conversational in nature, as I imagine us taking this journey of education together. We are not alone in our calling. We have a community of faith, strengthened with God-given gifts, insights, and passions! More powerful still, God who is Father, Son, and Holy Spirit, walks with us every step of the way.

Our devotional reflections are designed in the following format:

- A Guiding Passage: Bible verses and inspirational quotes have been selected to deepen and guide our reflection on the theme for the day. (You can find more information on the author or secondary source in the Notes section in the back of the book.)
- A Reflection: Our reflections will be in the form of stories, poems, guided questions, prayers, and thoughts for exploration and application.
- Intention Setting: You are invited to set an intention for each day. (If setting intentions is new to you, or if you would like to see some possible ideas, you can find a list of examples in the Going Deeper: Intentions section in the back of the book.)
- A Blessing: This is my personal prayer for your day.
- A Memorable Moment: At any point in your day, you are invited to write a memorable moment to remember in the future. Whether it is a surprising breakthrough for a student, or a silly conversation you overheard that you hope you will never forget, this is your space to capture those meaningful moments. (If you would like some inspiration on recording Memorable Moments, you can find a list of examples in the Going Deeper: Memorable Moments section in the back of the book.)

Thank you for joining me on this journey. You have been called to the classroom. Thank you for embracing this divine calling from God. As we set out on this adventure together, let us teach with passion and in community, rooted in Christ's love. With gritty faith, and a strong cup of coffee, anything can happen!

In love and faith, Christina

Additional Thoughts:

- Throughout our reflections together, you are invited to insert the identifiers for God which the Holy Spirit brings to your heart at that time. There may be verses, quotes, and reflections which lead you to name the Trinity as Mother (Isaiah 42:14), Friend (John 15:15), Shepherd (Psalm 23:1), Abba (Romans 8:15), and so on. I pray that as you read and reflect, God will be revealed to you in a personal, comforting way.
- As we begin our journey together, you may find it helpful to set apart a space and time to reflect with God. You may want a journal and pen handy for any thoughts or personal reflections you would like to add to this time. For me, my sacred time is in my car before the school day begins. I arrive at school several minutes early so I can sit in my car for my devotional time. My Bible, books, journal, and pens are always waiting on the passenger seat. You can make this look however it fits best into your life!

Part 1
I am Called

I AM CALLED

**"He has shown you, O mortal, what is good.
And what does the Lord require of you?
To act justly and to love mercy
and to walk humbly with your God."
~ Micah 6:8 (NIV)**

Do you have a central quote or verse that has supported you along your teaching journey? Perhaps a theme, motto, or mantra has grounded you in your learning space. As I completed my student teaching experience during my undergraduate education, Micah 6:8 became my, "teaching verse." Every time I read it, these holy words remind me of my calling: *Act justly. Love mercy. Walk humbly with God.*

We may be starting this year with the excitement of a child on their birthday, eager for a new year full of opportunities. Or perhaps, we woke up this morning feeling overwhelmed and anxious, contemplating the road before us. Most of us may find ourselves in between these feelings, optimistic for new growth and apprehensive about the work it will take to get there.

We have been called to a profession of unimaginable outcomes. Our Heavenly Teacher has incredible adventures in store for the days, weeks, and months to come. Let us step boldly forward into newness, rooted in our calling. God has placed us exactly where He has designed us to be.

Today's Intention:

_____

_____

_____

_____

May The Lord Bless You and Keep You:

Today, as you step into your space of learning, may you be called to make a difference.
May you be blessed with courage, so your actions protect and empower justice.
May you love mercy fiercely, even when mercy is mocked.
May you be willing to take risks in the name of learning and growing.
And may you take hold of God's hand and humbly walk with Him every step of the way.

Memorable Moment:

_____

_____

_____

_____

I AM A TEACHER

**"One child, one teacher, one book,
one pen can change the world.
Education is the only solution. Education first."
~ Malala Yousafzai [1]**

In case no one has told you today: Thank you. Thank you for every detail you have navigated in your personal and professional life to begin this school year. Whether you are setting out for the first time, navigating several years of experience, or approaching the end of your career, thank you for embarking on the adventure of teaching. I believe we have been called to the most influential profession in the world.

The Bible shares stories about teachers, mentors, and instructors. In many passages, this role is used as an example for our Christian lives. During His experience on earth, Jesus was an incredible teacher. Those who knew Him intimately and those who had only heard of His reputation referred to Him as Teacher. What a gift and an honor it is to share the title, position, and responsibility with Him. What an opportunity to change the world through our love and service.

As you enter your space of learning today, Jesus goes with you. Your influence can truly change the world as you follow His example of love. *Education first* means more than letters and numbers. Developing understanding begins with knowing one another, and the ability to empathize with lived experiences. Education invites a safe space for curiosity and individuality to be expressed, for goals to be set, and for endless opportunities to be sought. There are many challenges present in our world; perhaps *education is the only solution.*

Today's Intention:

_____

_____

_____

_____

May The Lord Bless You and Keep You:
Teacher, you were called and have answered the call.
Today, may you be blessed in your role as an educator and caregiver.
May you prayerfully overcome any feelings of inadequacy.
With a new perspective, may you see how impactful you are in the
lives of so many.
May the world be changed for the better: starting with you.

Memorable Moment:

_____

_____

_____

_____

I AM A WAYMAKER

"See, I am doing a new thing!
Now it springs up; do you not perceive it?
I am making a way in the wilderness
and streams in the wasteland."
~ Isaiah 19:43 (NIV)

A waymaker is one who goes ahead of others, creating opportunities for a way forward. Using their available resources to remove barriers and develop solutions, they take steps toward progress without knowing exactly what the journey will entail.

I cannot speak for all teachers and caregivers, but every year when the school year begins, I find myself gazing into what feels like an open expanse. There is a road ahead of me and my mind races with questions. *What will the student dynamics be? What lessons will be learned? What are the best approaches to support my students in their growth?* The adventurous side of me thrives in this mystery. The proactive organizer in me wants to throw up! Where do you land on this spectrum?

I am comforted by the words in our reflection verse for today, because they seem to portray both excitement and peace for those times when our learning spaces feel like a wilderness and wasteland. Be encouraged by Christ's ability to use challenging environments to make His way for us and those He has entrusted to us this year: *a way in the wilderness and streams in the wasteland.* By His example, we can begin to cultivate our spaces to prepare a way for each and every individual God has designed to be in our care. With our Heavenly Waymaker going before us, how will you create paths of learning and growth for your students?

Today's Intention:

_____

_____

_____

_____

May the Lord Bless You and Keep You:
Today, as you enter the sacred space of learning,
May you step forward in confidence, trusting your Maker has made a
way before you.
May your soul be awakened to what is awaiting you.
May your words, actions, and presence nourish those around you.
May you be blessed to be a waymaker.

Memorable Moment:

_____

_____

_____

_____

I AM EQUIPPED

"My dear children, you come from God and belong to God. You have already won a big victory over these false teachers, for the Spirit in you is far stronger than anything in the world."
~ 1 John 4:4 (MSG)

As we begin the school year, it is natural to think about the areas we are lacking. Our thoughts may linger to the items on the to-do lists we haven't checked off yet, or the classroom resources that were promised and never delivered. Perhaps the summer expectations, met or unmet, impact our mindsets about the coming days, weeks and months.

In the midst of these realities, God is continually equipping us. Through our experiences, conversations, and God-inspired reality, we possess more than we realize. Deeper still, we have the gift of the Holy Spirit to treasure and use in the areas we feel lacking. When I shift my focus towards our Heavenly Teacher and His power, I am amazed at what He reveals to me while I am teaching and learning with students.

There have been times when I would have responded too soon or in an unhelpful way, but I sensed a nudge to be still and listen. Other days, I felt led to pause and take time for a conversation with a student instead of rushing ahead to the next daily activity, resulting in building a foundation of trust between myself and the student. When we see the Holy Spirit as a part of the work we do in the classroom, we are more in tune with God's purpose and feel more equipped in our own lives.

Today's Intention:

_____

_____

_____

_____

May the Lord Bless You and Keep You:

Today, may you feel an extra sense of confidence as you rest in the truth that you are enough.
God has called and equipped you to do this meaningful work.
May you find the freedom to let go of some undone tasks.
May you stand strong in the power of knowing what God has begun, He will see to fruition.
And may you be inspired to equip and empower those around you.

Memorable Moment:

_____

_____

_____

_____

I AM NAMED

"But now, O Jacob, listen to the Lord who created you. O Israel, the one who formed you says, 'Do not be afraid, for I have ransomed you, I have called you by name; you are mine."
~ Isaiah 43:1 (NLT)

A practice in many classroom communities is a morning greeting. Whether this takes place by a teacher welcoming each student with a friendly, "Good morning!" in the hallway, or a meeting time when each student greets one another, a common theme is the use of names. The teacher greets the students by name. The students greet each other by name. In doing so, all participants feel seen, known, included, and loved.

Consider how it feels when we recognize Jesus calls us by our own name. We are seen, known, included, and unconditionally loved in His Kingdom. When we embrace this truth of belonging to our Heavenly Father - a child in His family - we are able to authentically embrace our students, the children God has called us to unconditionally love. We accept this gift with open arms so we may, in turn, open our arms to those around us.

Today, I invite you to reflect on your own name and identity in Christ. When you feel comfortable, express the following statements by inserting your name in the blank. (You may want to speak this out loud, say it in a whisper, or hold it closely in your heart.)

God, my Heavenly Father, speaks these words over me:

I have created you in My image, _____ .

I have formed you exactly as you are.

Do not be afraid, _____ , for I am with you.

I have called you by name, _____ . You are mine.

Today's Intention:

_____

_____

_____

_____

May the Lord **Bless You and Keep You:**

As you greet and gather today, may God share His perspective of His children with you.

May you cherish one another as unique, loved beings, designed in the image of Christ.

May you welcome those around you by name.

And may you step forward in the confidence that you are claimed and called. You are His.

Memorable Moment:

_____

_____

_____

_____

I AM CHOSEN

"It's in Christ that we find out who we are and what we are living for. Long before we first heard of Christ and got our hopes up, he had his eye on us, had designs on us for glorious living, part of the overall purpose he is working out in everything and everyone."
~ Ephesians 1:11-12 (MSG)

Think back to a time when someone picked you. Perhaps you were selected as a teammate, a partner, a position, or another type of role. What were some emotions you felt?

Our early memories of being chosen may have occurred at school. Being picked to share our writing, play on a team, or join the teacher for lunch are just a few examples. This act of being chosen subtly communicates that we are worthy, valuable, and have a purpose to contribute. Choosing each of our students is immensely powerful, a lasting impact we may not realize in the moment.

God chose you. He called you to be in the space you are in today. He saw value in your abilities, hard work, and passion. He has equipped you with everything you need at this time. In our questions of worthiness, we are reminded: *it's in Christ that we find out who we are and what we are living for*. Live in this truth today and invite others to live out their purposes as well.

Today's Intention:

_____

_____

_____

_____

May the Lord Bless You and Keep You:

You are chosen and unconditionally loved by God.
Today, stand grounded in this confidence.
You are not out of place.
May the Holy Spirit give you wisdom to choose someone else.
May you encourage a soul by explaining the value and purpose they
give to the world.
You may never know the outcome, but God will use this in
unimaginable ways.

Memorable Moment:

_____

_____

_____

_____

I AM INVITED

"And I ask him that with both feet planted firmly on love, you'll be able to take in with all followers of Jesus the extravagant dimensions of Christ's love. Reach out and experience the breadth! Test its length! Plumb the depths! Rise to the heights! Live full lives, full in the fullness of God."
~ Ephesians 3:17-19 (MSG)

The invitation to a new day.
Fresh starts all around.
What a demonstration of Grace!
A new day.

We enter this day,
Invited to leave behind the blemishes of yesterday.
Burdened and bruised, we search for healing.
Separated and saddened, we seek joy.
Grace meets us in the space between what was,
And what we hope will be.

With both feet planted firmly on love,
We create space for the extravagant dimensions of Christ's love.
He invites us to stretch,
Testing new muscles, abilities, and mindsets.
As we ask: how far does this Love extend?
Now it is time to decide:
Will we also invite others to start fresh?
A new day!

Today's Intention:

_____

_____

_____

_____

May the Lord Bless You and Keep You:

Today, may you be invited into a new beginning.
May the Holy Spirit fill you with the capacity to take in the extravagant
dimensions of Christ's love.
May you reach out and experience the breadth of His plan for your life.
May you decide each day to live a full life, full in the fullness of God!
May you invite others into a life of abundance, feet planted firmly on love.

Memorable Moment:

_____

_____

_____

_____

I AM AN INCLUDER

"Then he said to them, 'Whoever welcomes this little child in my name welcomes me; and whoever welcomes me welcomes the one who sent me. For it is the one who is least among you all who is the greatest.'"
~ Luke 9:48 (NIV)

What an incredible feeling to be included. Truly included. No expectations or standards attached. Our loving Father has created each person to be included in His family, making us children of God. His divine design includes all people. Imagine what the world would be like if more families, churches, schools, and communities viewed inclusion in this way. Truly included.

If we allow ourselves to honestly reflect, we might acknowledge there are individuals who are easier to invite into our lives and spend time with, because they feel natural, comfortable, and relatable. They bring something to the table that makes us feel at ease. Similarly, individuals who feel challenging to include may come to mind as well. Perhaps they are complicated, needy, or just downright stressful. (Yes, we're keeping it real today because our very real God knows our hearts and minds.) Let's think of our families, administrators, colleagues, and students. Who are we naturally including and excluding?

We are not responsible for anyone's response to an invitation. But we *are* responsible for extending the invitation. Our loving Father has included us in our best moments and in our worst. When we are joyfully serving and when we make mistakes, we are still truly included. He calls us to share the same invitation with others.

Today's Intention:

_____

_____

_____

_____

May the Lord Bless You and Keep You:
You are included. You have a place in God's family no one can take.
In your days of loneliness, you will never have to face isolation when you
accept this loving invitation.
Filled with love, may you extend a warm welcome to those around you.
May you have eyes to see the invisible ones in your midst.
May you have ears to hear the gentle whispers or loud anger of loneliness.
And may you have the strength to respond with unconditional inclusivity.

Memorable Moment:

_____

_____

_____

_____

I AM A CULTIVATOR

"The task of the modern educator is not to cut down jungles, but to irrigate deserts."
~ C.S. Lewis [2]

Cultivation is the process of preparing soil to be a strong place for growth. It involves removing and destroying weeds to promote aeration, so water and air can move throughout the dirt. To me, the first several days and weeks of a school year feel like a season of cultivation. We, as educators and mentors, are extremely intentional in creating space for learning and growth. We prepare to raise and uplift those in our care.

This preparation requires loosening what was: habits formed, expectations of perfection, and preconceived notions of what will be. We foster growth by ensuring our soil (the culture of our classroom) is full of rich nutrients. And we work intently, care unconditionally, and study curiously to push ourselves and our students toward growth.

How thankful I am that Our Heavenly Gardener has cultivated in us a passion for young people. We have been prepared and fostered, perpetually improved by the Creator who makes our growth possible. And yes, through this process, we have most likely felt broken in some ways. Harmful weeds are in the process of being removed and destroyed to make way for growth. Christ is with us in our brokenness because, unlike any other, He sees and understands what we face. He continues to stand with us as we move forward, cultivating growth, and loving those we encounter each day.

Today's Intention:

_____

_____

_____

_____

May the Lord Bless You and Keep You:

As you consider the openness and opportunity of the soil before you today, may God give you wisdom to cultivate a space of belonging and grace.
May you prayerfully consider what you may need to break hold of in order to find growth and peace.
May you be inspired to work hard, love deeply, and remain curious.
May you radiate Christ's light in the lives of all around you.

Memorable Moment:

_____

_____

_____

_____

I AM A COMMUNITY-BUILDER

"Forming community goes straight to the heart of what makes our work so rewarding: It is where connection and joy lay."
~ Elena Aguilar [3]

Our classroom communities are sacred spaces. "Community" is a common word that circulates as the school year begins. We are engaging in social-emotional learning conversations and framing our classroom routines, and yet, in all the busyness, we may forget to slow down and reflect on what authentic community means and how it feels. Let's take a moment to do this together. Feel free to jot down some notes as we consider these questions:

What does community look like to you?

When have you been a part of a healthy, encouraging community?

What characteristics or actions were foundational in building this

group and space?

We have been given a rich task of creating the space for strengthening friendships, developing respect, and recognizing the dignity and value within each person. There may be students who have never experienced being a part of a healthy group that is dedicated to their progress and potential. We have an opportunity to make this a reality in their lives. What a powerful opportunity this is!

Today's Intention:

_____

_____

_____

_____

May the Lord Bless You and Keep You:

May God richly bless your space of learning and all who step into it.
May connections be formed and values respected.
May strengths be uplifted and growth inspired.
May every person who enters feel seen and valued for who they are.
And may you be blessed to build this strong community.

Memorable Moment:

_____

_____

_____

_____

I AM LOVED

"Watch what God does, and then you do it, like children who learn proper behavior from their parents. Mostly what God does is love you. Keep company with him and learn a life of love. Observe how Christ loved us. His love was not cautious but extravagant. He didn't love in order to get something from us but to give everything of himself to us. Love like that."
~ Ephesians 5:1-2 (MSG)

Not cautious but extravagant.

Our world is filled with cautious expressions of love. We have risked vulnerable, extravagant love before and experienced hurt, so we promise ourselves we will be more careful next time. We have poured every last ounce of care and compassion into that *one* student and saw no growth, so we vow to care a little less next year to protect our precious bank of energy.

Observe how Christ loved us.

When He walked this earth, Jesus did not imitate the cautious expressions of love. In the Gospels, we read story after story of how He bent down and lifted up, healed with His muddy hands, advocated for the outcast, and invited to the table those who would be turned away by others.

We know worldly love because we feel it daily. It is conditional. It is painful. It is sitting alone in our hurt wondering if someone will only reach out when we have mustered the strength to pick ourselves up first. But what if that pattern could change? What if it starts with you and me today, loving those around us extravagantly and taking another risk. After all, Christ risked everything for us.

Today's Intention:

_____

_____

_____

_____

May the Lord Bless You and Keep You:

You are loved, my friend.
On the days you don't feel it, or cannot believe it, you are still loved.
May you be open to embracing that extravagant love today.
Out of this powerful love, may you love those around you
unconditionally.
By this world-changing expression of love, may you bring glory and
honor to our example: Jesus.

Memorable Moment:

_____

_____

_____

_____

I AM KNOWN

**"My sheep listen to my voice;
I know them, and they follow me."
~ John 10:27 (NIV)**

How incredible it is to feel known! In our lives of faith, the essence of being known transcends knowledge alone. It is to be in a place of vulnerability and safety simultaneously, understood and loved for exactly who we are. We are known and deeply cared for by our Heavenly Teacher. Our deepest fears and insecurities, our past experiences and future possibilities, our quirks, passions, and dreams - Jesus knows them all! In this verse from John's gospel, first the Shepherd *knows* His sheep, and then they follow Him. I believe the order is purposeful. Being seen, known, and valued is a prerequisite to trust, faith, and obedience. Belonging is an intrinsic desire within all people.

At the beginning of the school year, we are invited to create a culture where our students and colleagues are known and have value. Let's reflect on several questions to consider how we can create spaces of deep connection and understanding.

Do your students and colleagues feel known by you?

Do we know our students' interests and goals?

Can we recognize what makes them anxious, fearful, or turned off

completely?

By simply looking into their eyes, can we decipher their mood?

How do you think every classroom, every hallway, every school and district would be transformed if students entered into their space of learning and felt truly known? I've seen this atmosphere in many classrooms, and it produces powerful outcomes. God is calling us to create these safe places for our students to feel known and valued. This is the most important work.

Today's Intention:

_____

_____

_____

_____

May the Lord Bless You and Keep You:

Today, may you feel known and unconditionally loved.
From this Truth, may you be inspired to get to know those around
you in a deeper way.
May you ask questions, listen intently, and point out areas of strength.
May all who enter your room feel safe, known, and valued.
And may others draw closer to our Heavenly Father because of your
words and actions.

Memorable Moment:

_____

_____

_____

_____

I AM ROOTED

"So then, just as you received Christ Jesus as Lord, continue to live your lives in him, rooted and built up in him, strengthened in the faith as you were taught, and overflowing with thankfulness."
~ Colossians 2:6-7 (NIV)

Let's consider roots today. I love having plants around me, planting seeds and hoping for growth. However, this is an area I am still developing as I often struggle to keep plants alive. Through my horticultural missteps, I have discovered the importance of space and soil. Before seeds are even planted, creating enough space for future growth sets them up for success. Additionally, choosing soil rich with nutrients will strengthen the growing plant. Of course, the correct amount of water and sunlight is also needed. When the roots are strong, the plant is more successful. Without a doubt, supporting these strong roots requires effort and intentionality.

Strengthening our faith roots is no different. Space and nourishment are necessary for trust to grow. The beginning of the school year is a powerful time to create space to cultivate our faith. Setting aside time to pray and meditate on God's Word sustains our soul and prepares us for what may come later. In difficult times, we will stand strong because we are rooted and built up in Christ.

In our classrooms, this is also a time when students are developing roots. They are building a foundation for this year and years to come. We are called to create an atmosphere in which students are given the opportunities to grow, take risks, and thrive in a safe environment. Their roots will strengthen as we provide support and encouragement. As the year progresses, we will remain faithful to them as Christ has been faithful to us.

Today's Intention:

_____

_____

_____

_____

May the Lord Bless You and Keep You:

*Today, may you be connected deeply to Christ, rooted in His love.
May the Holy Spirit build up and strengthen you for the work you
have been called to do.
Grounded in God's faithfulness, may you cultivate space and
nourishment for your students to grow.
And in the midst of your busy day, may your soul overflow with
thankfulness for all the ways God has been fruitful in your life.*

Memorable Moment:

_____

_____

_____

_____

I AM INTENTIONAL

**"Careful planning puts you ahead in the long run;
Hurry and scurry puts you further behind."
~ Proverbs 21:5 (MSG)**

We are in the midst of a season of intentional planning. The groundwork we are laying in the first weeks of school is incredibly valuable in shaping the atmosphere of our learning spaces. As we balance the many responsibilities in front of us, be it professional or personal, the tasks seem to quickly and subtly multiply. How do we catch our breath, regain focus, and maintain intentionality in our practice? We have written the lists, prioritized calendars, sacrificed precious moments, and prayed for wisdom.

I won't pretend I have the answer to this question; however, a perspective which has grounded me is consistent reflection on *Who* has called me to this work and *who* I am called to serve. God has purposed us for this work, so we can be intentional by reflecting on the tasks that will bring honor to Him. Our purpose is to be present for our students.

Which responsibilities bring a direct, positive impact to our learners? Of course, there will always be necessary logistical tasks, but we can choose to limit the emotional energy we invest in these. Then we can find freedom in developing intentionality, using our time and talents for what truly matters: the students in our midst. And at the end of the day, we trust God with the rest.

Today's Intention:

_____

_____

_____

_____

May the Lord Bless You and Keep You:
Today, may God inspire wisdom and discernment.
May you be guided away from tasks and conversations that do not serve a greater purpose.
May you use your creativity in ways that invigorate your heart and encourage your learners.
And may your intentionality empower a strong foundation for the future.

Memorable Moment:

_____

_____

_____

_____

I AM A PLANNER

**"It is not enough for the teacher to love the child.
She must first love and understand the universe.
She must prepare herself, and truly work at it."
~ Maria Montessori** [4]

Our faith is one of conviction, passion, and courage. Choosing to follow God's calling into education is not for the faint of heart. As we have reflected, it requires us to be relational, loving, and rooted in our identity. I believe God is calling us to be experts, learning and rehearsing academic content and pedagogy. We are knowledgeable about child development, social and emotional risk factors, and positive communication methods.

We are also intentional planners. This is an aspect of our calling designed by God, our omnipotent Planner. An expert educator seeks to create an atmosphere of safety, where boundaries are understood and consistent. When we plan lessons, we proactively anticipate where students may have misconceptions, or where the energy and engagement may lag. We look for exciting ways to make learning fascinating and personal because that is truly what all learning should be.

Teaching and learning is our craft, and we are invited to embrace our professionalism in it. However, raising the expectations of how and what we teach is not simple! To live out our teaching practice in this way means we are almost always swimming upstream. Who is swimming with us? Family, friends, colleagues, or leadership? If someone who mirrors this dedication does not come to mind, consider how we might widen our circle. Furthermore, we remember Jesus' example as a teacher. He loves and understands the universe. He prepared Himself for His calling and truly worked at it! We are not alone.

Today's Intention:

_____

_____

_____

_____

May the Lord Bless You and Keep You:
May you intentionally look ahead at what you can control.
In these areas, may the Holy Spirit give you discernment and creativity in planning.
May you take a courageous step forward and stand out from the crowd for the sake of your calling.
May you not fear others' perceptions of you, but keep your eyes focused on your Savior.
You are called to purposeful tasks today.
Honor them with your energy.

Memorable Moment:

_____

_____

_____

_____

I AM AMBITIOUS

"...I want you to get out there and walk - better yet, run! - on the road God called you to travel. I don't want any of you sitting around on your hands. I don't want anyone strolling off, down some path that goes nowhere. And mark that you do this with humility and discipline - not in fits and starts, but steadily, pouring yourselves out for each other in acts of love, alert at noticing differences and quick at mending fences."
~ Ephesians 4:1-3 (MSG)

Sometimes we never know in life.
We wake up in the morning; God's mercies new and fresh.
Days and weeks are ahead; anything can happen.
New ideas are forming and goals emerging.
We don't know what's around the corner,
Whose life we could impact next,
Or what new adventure we will embark upon.
In the mystery, we set out in humility and discipline
To chase the dream God has set before us.
We are ambitious!

The exciting, yet at times daunting reality is:
We serve an ambitious God!
Called by God and rooted in His purpose,
We become more powerful than we could have ever imagined.
Remember to work hard and be kind.
Run hard to stay on the road God has called you to travel.
Be focused.
You are never guaranteed another day or opportunity.
Do justice. Love mercy. Walk humbly with God.
Today is the day the Lord has made! Let us live it ambitiously!

Today's Intention:

_____

_____

_____

_____

May the Lord Bless You and Keep You:

As you prepare for the day ahead, may you find new energy to run the path God has put before you.
May you be humble and treat others with gracious love.
May you be self-disciplined and proud of your determination.
And may you notice each child of God as unique and worthy of belonging.

Memorable Moment:

_____

_____

_____

_____

I AM LIGHT

**"In the same way, let your light shine before others,
that they may see your good deeds and glorify your Father in
heaven."
~ Matthew 5:16 (NIV)**

Light is diverse.

Light is a sunrise, illuminating a busy city.

Light is one lit candle in an empty, dark room.

Light is a movie on a big screen, projecting stories to be

seen and heard.

Light is the joy of twinkle lights.

Light is a lantern exploring unknown paths.

Light is the headlights of a car bringing a loved one home.

Light is a sunset over the ocean.

Light is a million stars, scattered and energetic.

Light is a searchlight, scanning the seas for danger.

We are called to be Light in this world.

This may look unique to each of us,

Because Light is designed to take different forms.

What is your God-given Light?

Today's Intention:

_____

_____

_____

_____

May the Lord Bless You and Keep You:

Today, may you have eyes to see yourself and others in a new Light.
May you embrace the Light you have been given.
May you let your Light shine in the midst of others, so they may see
your impact, giving God glory.
May you see the Light in those around you and inspire them to shine
even brighter.

Memorable Moment:

_____

_____

_____

_____

I AM MOTIVATED

"If the goals you are pursuing are centered only on serving you, you will likely compromise at some point. If you are pursuing goals centered on becoming who God called you to be, you will be unwavering in your pursuit."
~ Sydney Stephens [5]

Motivation is often considered to be a mood - we either feel motivated or we don't. However, I believe when we are rooted and strengthened in Christ, motivation becomes an intrinsic characteristic instead of a passing feeling. Reflect for a moment on who or what inspires you. What gets you out of bed in the morning and brings you peace at night?

Our faith stirs in us the strength and love for children who are not given a voice, a chance, or an opportunity. The ones who weep, and no one sees. The ones who yell, and no one hears. These are God's children - God's babies. They hold their arms up in anticipation, and we move closer and pick them up. We are motivated because we understand our students cannot afford mediocrity.

Today, we are motivated to be in this place. Right here. Right now. We are motivated to be the Light. We are motivated to build up, inspire, believe, and display hope. We are confident that, even in the midst of chaos, we are claimed, held, and strengthened by God: equipped for our calling. We will not be moved from our roots.

Today's Intention:

_____

_____

_____

_____

May the Lord Bless You and Keep You:

Today, may you feel a fresh, motivating breath of energy.
You are called and equipped to do the impossible.
May you be blessed with surprising bursts of joy.
May you be rooted and strong in the face of your adversaries -
whatever form they may be.
And may you rest tonight, embracing the freedom of Christ's
unconditional love.

Memorable Moment:

_____

_____

_____

_____

I AM VALUED

"When a child walks into the room, your child or anybody else's child, do your eyes light up?
That's what they're looking for."
~ Toni Morrison [6]

Our school year is well underway, and the realness is setting in. We are most likely restating expectations and rehearsing routines more than anticipated. It has been a blink of an eye and already formal assessments are fast approaching. Our calendars are filled with meetings and conferences. All the while, those beautiful and frightening true colors are making an appearance like the turning colors of autumn leaves. And I don't just mean your students' colors. *Your* colors, your *colleagues'* colors, the *parents'* colors. It's all happening.

We may even begin to question our own actions and abilities. *Am I really cut out for this?* God answers our deep wonderings with a resounding, "Yes!" God's eyes light up when He sees you. Your spirit and gifts, time and energy, and love and devotion are irreplaceable. You are more valuable than you will ever know.

I wonder if our students ever have these questions too. What are our students looking for? In all of our to-do lists, calendars, and lesson plans, do we find the answer? In the midst of our complex professional demands, we can find comfort knowing the truth is really quite simple: *Do your eyes light up? That's what they're looking for.*

Today's Intention:

_____

_____

_____

_____

May the Lord Bless You and Keep You:
You are precious in God's sight.
You hold incomprehensible value to Him.
May you embrace your own worth, so you may truly value others.
As you enter your classroom today, may you refocus your priorities.
May your interactions with those around you communicate authentic
messages of worth and belonging.
In the midst of the chaos, may your eyes light up when someone steps
through the door.

Memorable Moment:

_____

_____

_____

_____

I AM CLAIMED

"For in him we live and move and have our being."
~ Acts 17:28a (NIV)

In our previous reflection, we explored the importance of valuing the students God has placed in our midst. But I have come to believe, it is virtually impossible to truly value others if we struggle to value ourselves. If we cannot unconditionally embrace ourselves in all our imperfection and messiness, how can we welcome those around us?

I'll admit it is difficult to understand and fully accept God's love for me. It goes against my human nature to believe God loves me apart from my works. In a society where our actions and performance seem to dictate our worth, receiving a contrary method of love sometimes feels uncomfortable and foreign. But this is Truth: We are claimed by God.

In Him, we live and move, and have our being.

In our personal and professional lives, we are pulled in many directions. However, we can rest in knowing that, when we are rooted in Christ, this is where we belong, and we are claimed. He will not change. He will not fail.

Today's Intention:

_____

_____

_____

_____

May the Lord Bless You and Keep You:
Today, you are claimed.
You are claimed no matter what you produce.
You are claimed regardless of the score on the assessment.
You are claimed when you are tired and when you have energy.
You are claimed when you cry and when you laugh.
You are unconditionally claimed.

Memorable Moment:

_____

_____

_____

_____

I AM BLESSED

**"Whatever is good and perfect is a gift coming down to us from God our Father, who created all the lights in the heavens. He never changes or casts a shifting shadow."
~ James 1:17 (NLT)**

God, our Creator,
We praise You for the gifts you provide:
For water, shelter, comfort, and beauty;
For the students you have placed in our care and direction;
For the energy, strength, and perseverance to be an educator.
We are generously blessed.

Jesus, our constant Companion,
We thank you for Your presence, so we are never alone or misunderstood.
You walk with us each step of the journey.
You share in our joys, sorrows, celebrations, and hurts.
You know our experiences, told and untold.
We are compassionately cared for.

Holy Spirit, Light in and through us,
We breathe in the fresh air of Your Life, and we are grateful.
You excite our souls and challenge our mindsets.
You inspire new ideas rooted in love, and caution patterns that have acted as a barrier to love.
You guide our conversations to uplift and encourage.
We are humbled, filled with joy, and so very blessed.

Today's Intention:

_____

_____

_____

_____

May the Lord Bless You and Keep You:
Today, may you feel overwhelmingly blessed!
May you reflect on the experiences you have been given, shaping you into who you are.
In gratitude, may you be mindful of God's provision over your life.
May your day be full of praise opportunities, thanking God for the people surrounding you.
May you be blessed to be a blessing to others.

Memorable Moment:

_____

_____

_____

_____

I AM SAVED

**"From the ends of the earth I call to you,
I call as my heart grows faint; lead me to the rock that is higher
than I."
~ Psalm 61:2 (NIV)**

In our reflections, we have explored our calling and God's design in choosing us for this work. We have embraced our ambition, excitement, and motivation, knowing we are rooted in Christ above all else. These are important pieces of who we are and Whose we are. To build on these discussions, let's explore our deepest foundation: we are saved. We are who we are because of Who we believe in. Our relationship with Jesus Christ empowers us to live out this calling of service and advocacy.

Hear this today: Jesus has saved you from the condemnation of others, and the lies Satan would have you believe. He has saved you from trying to dig your way out of past mistakes or difficult circumstances. With His very life, He has reached down to the deepest depths to search for you, and to climb back up with you. There is nothing separating you from His unconditional love.

We will have moments when we trip up, fall on our face, and make a mess. We will have days when we feel so incredibly exhausted or heartbroken, we don't know how we will continue. Jesus reaches further than these places, just to make sure He is fully with us. He saves us, yesterday, today, and forever.

Today's Intention:

_____

_____

_____

_____

May the Lord Bless You and Keep You:
May you humbly embrace the need for your Savior.
May Jesus enter into your learning space in a personal way today.
May you be an advocate and caregiver, knowing you are deeply
advocated and cared for.
May shame and guilt have no place in your thoughts, actions, or heart.
You are saved.

Memorable Moment:

_____

_____

_____

_____

I AM ANOINTED

"The Spirit of the Sovereign Lord is on me, because the Lord has anointed me to proclaim good news to the poor. He has sent me to bind up the brokenhearted, to proclaim freedom for the captives, and release from darkness for the prisoners."
~ Isaiah 61:1 (NIV)

Today, in the midst of all the chaos, I would like to invite you to pause and imagine entering into your space of work. But you are not alone. Jesus is walking beside you, with a small bag in his hand. You are making your way through the halls to your classroom or office. Once you open the door and turn on the lights, immediately your thoughts run through all the tasks you need to accomplish before the workday actually starts. Your eyes are looking around the room, your hands grabbing for to-do lists.

Quietly, Jesus walks toward you and gently touches your hand as it frantically searches for lost papers. You pause, turn, and look into His understanding eyes. For a moment, you had forgotten He arrived with you. He takes your hand and peacefully leads you to the center of the room. From the bag in His hand, He takes out a jar. Pouring a small amount of oil on His fingers, Jesus looks into your eyes, and makes the sign of the cross on your head with the oil.

"I have anointed you for this Good work, my friend," He says, in a loving, powerful voice. "You are here today to be My hands and feet: binding up the brokenhearted, inspiring freedom, and sharing Light. I have equipped you for this purpose. And I will never leave you alone in this calling."

Today's Intention:

_____

_____

_____

_____

May the Lord Bless You and Keep You:
May you walk with the purpose of one anointed.
Remember that you have been chosen, sought after, valued, and called.
May Jesus walk with you today, pausing your distractions to anoint you again.
You are not here by chance. You did not make a mistake.
You are anointed. Walk forward in this Truth.

Memorable Moment:

_____

_____

_____

_____

I AM COVERED

**"He will cover you with his feathers, and under his wings you
will find refuge;
his faithfulness will be your shield and rampart."
~ Psalm 91:4 (NIV)**

On the days we need it the most,

God's love envelops us like a warm blanket,

Covering every part of who we are,

Protecting us from the outside elements,

Providing safety and comfort.

God's unconditional love covers:

Our fears, mistakes, and questions;

Our hurts, uncertainties, and shame;

Our loneliness and unworthiness;

Our life.

God's unconditional love covers:

Our desires, hopes, and dreams;

Our potential, passions, and goals;

Our family, friends, and students;

There is no space or place God's love does not cover.

Today's Intention:

_____

_____

_____

_____

May the Lord Bless You and Keep You:
Today, may you feel the incomprehensible peace of God.
May you sense His surpassing love over your life.
May your mind and heart be covered by the blood of Jesus Christ.
And when questions and doubts form, may you come before God in
prayer and thanksgiving for His protection over you.

Memorable Moment:

_____

_____

_____

_____

I AM PROACTIVE

"But seek first his kingdom and his righteousness, and all these things will be given to you as well. Therefore do not worry about tomorrow, for tomorrow will worry about itself. Each day has enough trouble of its own."
~ Matthew 6:33-34 (NIV)

In Stephen Covey's popular book, "The 7 Habits of Highly Effective People," the first habit he outlines is: Be Proactive.[7] He discusses the difference between being proactive and reactive. In other words, how do we handle the expected or unexpected challenges that show up in our day? Do we feel anxious and out of control, or are we able to maintain calm and stay grounded?

Perhaps, our reflection verses do not seem to accurately parallel the theme of being proactive. After all, proactive means to think ahead, right? And yet, we read, *Do not worry about tomorrow, for tomorrow will worry about itself.* If we understand proactivity as setting ourselves up for emotional success by not becoming derailed every time something unexpected happens, then we need to dig deeper than our to-do lists and perfect lesson plans.

The proactive part of these verses is: *Seek first His kingdom.* It may sound simple and overstated; however, I believe when we are nourished by God's Word and communicate with Him consistently, there are proactive outcomes we may not even anticipate! We make decisions with more clarity. We show more authentic compassion to those around us. Above all, we remain grounded in our purpose and calling.

Today's Intention:

_____

_____

_____

_____

May the Lord Bless You and Keep You:

May you enter your space of calling with a trusting spirit.
May you begin today centered on Christ's love and provision for you.
When interruptions occur, may you have a spirit of patience and gracious understanding.
May you be proactive in seeking Jesus above all else.
And may you have the discipline to take it one day at a time, committing the future to God.

Memorable Moment:

_____

_____

_____

_____

I AM A LEADER

"Daring leadership is leading from heart, not hurt."
~ Brené Brown [8]

Do you consider yourself a leader? Why or why not?

Really think about this question for a moment.

What an honorable responsibility it is to be called to a position of leadership in our work and communities. We may not always feel like leaders. Perhaps, we envision a leader as a specific historical figure or someone who holds a position of power in our society. I push back against those limitations. To me, being a leader means living with integrity and grit in the here and now. Leaders are influential, and the results can be positive or negative.

How are we showing up as leaders?

The way we consistently conduct ourselves results in how we show up as a leader. I believe authentic leadership has nothing to do with comparing ourselves to others, and everything to do with how we focus and stay in our respective lanes. We are models of Christ's example when others witness our genuine kindness and call to action, removing distractions of gossiping and complaining. When those around us feel seen and valued by us, this is evidence of strong leadership. Even more importantly, this is how we are seen as one called by Christ, giving Him all the glory.

Today's Intention:

_____

_____

_____

_____

May the Lord Bless You and Keep You:
You are a leader.
May you feel empowered by God's strength to live out this role with honor and integrity.
May your words and actions inspire others to be the best they can be.
When you feel ill-equipped, may the Holy Spirit fill you with grace and power.
And may impactful leaders spring forth around you, advocating for justice in His Kingdom today.

Memorable Moment:

_____

_____

_____

_____

I AM PROFESSIONAL

"Stay calm; mind your business; do your own job. ...We want you living in a way that will command the respect of outsiders, not lying around sponging off your friends."
~ 1 Thessalonians 4:11-12 (MSG)

Real Talk Time. This is a phrase I use in my classroom when we need to have a conversation about something that may be challenging, but will, ultimately, make our community stronger. Even though our reflection verses were originally intended for a Thessalonian audience, it feels like the Apostle Paul is giving us a *Real Talk Time* as well.

We may teach in a space that does not provide a healthy work environment for our mind, body, and spirit. Consider the daily conversations among your colleagues. Is the general outcome one of encouragement and empathetic listening? Is productive problem-solving happening? Or are most of the in-between discussions focused on complaining and gossiping? Perhaps there is a combination of both, depending on the time of year and who is taking part in the dialogue.

In my experience, I've found, after managing my patience with students and juggling so many demands of the day, complaining to my colleague does not actually make me feel any better. Asking someone else to do a task for me doesn't make me feel any less busy. I think this is why Paul gave this advice to Christ-followers. It is not a rule to add to our rulebook, but instead wisdom to help us remain focused in our calling. We are professionals, and sometimes that means stepping up, showing up, and not conforming to others' patterns of conversation and behavior. After all, we are called and equipped to be Christ's light.

Today's Intention:

_____

_____

_____

_____

May the Lord Bless You and Keep You:

Today, may you step up and own the role of a professional in your field. You have spent time, effort, and creativity to be in the position you have been called to.

May you rise above thoughts, talk, and actions that would diminish the importance of your purpose.

May you conduct yourself in a manner which inspires others to rise up also.

May you be a change-agent for the community and culture of your workspace.

Memorable Moment:

_____

_____

_____

_____

I AM AN EXPERT

**"The mediocre teacher tells.
The good teacher explains.
The superior teacher demonstrates.
The great teacher inspires."
~ William Arthur Ward** [9]

How often do you feel ill-equipped to do this job? Have you had days this year when you just sat there after the end of a long day and thought, "I wasn't meant to do this"? Or, "It'll never be enough"? If you can relate to these experiences, I want you to know you are not alone.

Sometimes, I wonder if a reason we feel this way is because we are great teachers held to mediocre standards. Most curriculum is designed to *tell* and *explain*. Some schools are blessed to have the resources of time and materials to *demonstrate*. Ultimately, it is up to us to create *inspiration*. We are equipped to take on this challenge as we are developing as experts in our field.

Inspiration in teaching is made from two ingredients: a passion for what we're teaching and a love for our students. What if we aren't enthusiastic about the unit we're teaching? We need to figure it out. As experts, we need to find something about that Algebra unit that we can take and run with for the sake of our students. It may be challenging, but inspiration often requires authenticity and struggle. Remember, we are teaching out of love and concern for our students. Think of how many people you have heard say something to the effect of, "I really liked my seventh-grade teacher because he was a huge history nerd! I never really cared about history, but I loved his class because he was so passionate about history, and he genuinely cared about us." You have that opportunity today. Who might your expertise inspire?

Today's Intention:

_____

_____

_____

_____

May the Lord Bless You and Keep You:
Today, may God inspire your heart and mind with a new idea.
May you take a risk in the name of students and learning.
May old habits be evaluated, and new opportunities explored.
May God place learners in your space who will be inspired to make
the world a better place.
With God, all things are possible.

Memorable Moment:

_____

_____

_____

_____

I AM POSITIVE

"Do everything readily and cheerfully - no bickering, no second-guessing allowed! Go out into the world uncorrupted, a breath of fresh air in this squalid and polluted society. Provide people with a glimpse of good living and the living God."
~ Philippians 2:14-15 (MSG)

I want to express right away: this reflection is not going to be a "fake it 'til you make it" positivity plan. This can work for a time, but ultimately is not sustainable, nor very uplifting. Instead, we are inspired by the Apostle Paul's wisdom on remaining positive in all we do. Keep in mind, Paul had endured unimaginable abuse, torture, and ongoing hardship for the sake of his calling. He understood what suffering feels like.

Through this understanding, he gave the Philippians (and us today) a picture of the emotional outcomes of following Jesus. It may be difficult to hear, but bickering, complaining, and gossiping don't actually get us closer to where we want to be. Paul wanted us to be closer to our goals!

When others are with us, we should feel like *a breath of fresh air*. A person who is putting on a mask of cheerful positivity has nothing fresh about them. But someone who finds authentic joy in small moments, focuses on the task at hand, and offers gratitude to those around them is a burst of life on an otherwise mediocre day. Being on the lookout for God's blessings and developing a mindset of thankfulness are two powerful steps to developing authentic positivity.

Today's Intention:

_____

_____

_____

_____

May the Lord Bless You and Keep You:

Today is the day the Lord has made.
May you rejoice and be glad in it!
May you have eyes to see and ears to hear the unexpected blessings
God has placed in your day.
May you be a breath of fresh air to your learners and colleagues.
May you be blessed to be a blessing.

Memorable Moment:

_____

_____

_____

_____

I AM A BELIEVER

"For we live by believing and not by seeing."
~ 2 Corinthians 5:7 (NLT)

Dear _____,

I believe in you.

I believe in you on your strongest and on your weakest days.
I believe in you when you are excited and passionate!
I believe in you when you have given up.

I believe in you when you feel hurt and angry.
I believe in you when it is hard to find hope again.
I believe in you when trust has been broken.

I believe in you when you are uncertain.
I believe in you when you don't have every detail figured out.
I believe in you when you get it wrong a few times.

I believe in you when you take risks.
I believe in you when you lean on others.
I believe in you when you are vulnerable.
I believe in you when you are uniquely *you*.

Go and do likewise.

Love, God
Sincerely, Your Teacher
With Care, This Author

Today's Intention:

_____

_____

_____

_____

May the Lord Bless You and Keep You:

May you begin this day in the confident Truth that God believes in you.
He has called you for this purpose and believes in you every step of the way.
May the Holy Spirit strengthen your faith so failures do not define your worth or potential.
May you deeply believe in others.
May your belief in others strengthen your community and bring Light.

Memorable Moment:

_____

_____

_____

_____

Part 2
I Am Connected

I AM CONNECTED

"We're hardwired for connection - it's what gives purpose and meaning to our lives. The absence of love, belonging, and connection always leads to suffering."
~ Brené Brown [10]

I'm not sure if I will ever think of the word "connection" in the same way again. After the coronavirus reshaped the world (starting in late 2019), the idea of connection has taken on a whole new meaning. I remember being so thankful for Spring Break in March 2020; as the students left the building, my colleagues and I waved to them saying, "Have a great break! See you in a week!" We were looking forward to a much-needed time of rest, as well. We had no idea we would be welcoming the students back via a screen instead of in the classrooms.

The following year, my teaching position was completely virtual. Like so many others in our world, I felt an abrupt loneliness - a kind I had never experienced before. In my search for connection and belonging, my understanding of God's love, comfort, and nearness increased. The promise to draw near to God and He will draw near to me (James 4:8) became authentic and real in my life. Out of this relationship with my Heavenly Father, I decided the most important objective for every day of that school year would be to cultivate connection. Creating a classroom community of over twenty third-graders in a virtual setting was a new, uncharted task to say the least, but we did it.

I share this story because I imagine it feels familiar and relatable. During this time, the entire world received an amazing lesson in the vitality of meaningful connections with those around us. Let's not forget the lessons we've learned. No matter our role, if we influence the lives of children and young adults, we should invest in connection every day. There may be students who have never felt connected the way they do at school or in our classrooms. Despite the countless expectations put upon us, we can choose to prioritize connection. It is contagious and beautiful.

Today's Intention:

_____

_____

_____

_____

May the Lord Bless You and Keep You:

Today, may you feel an intimate connection with your loving Father.
May you reflect on those you are close to and be thankful for them.
May you be courageous in creating a space of connection.
And may you have opportunities to pause and watch connections
grow and spread around you.

Memorable Moment:

_____

_____

_____

_____

I AM RELATIONAL

"Anyone who welcomes you welcomes me, and anyone who welcomes me welcomes the one who sent me."
~ Matthew 10:40 (NIV)

Most likely as educators, one of our core strengths is the ability to connect with others. Perhaps we entered this field because we are able to build strong relationships. However, possessing strength in an area does not free us from difficulty. The very essence of being relational is to be vulnerable. We open ourselves up to others and risk whatever positive or negative impact this brings.

At times, we may wonder if it's worth it. Is it worth investing so much time, energy, and love when we may never see the results? I have witnessed teachers who have become numb to forming relationships with students and colleagues. Maybe we have had days when we feel the numbing begin. It seems easier to avoid all feelings so we can simply do the next thing. But I believe it is the relational component of our jobs that pushes us to keep moving forward. This may be what gets us out of bed in the morning.

God created us to be relational human beings. We are living out God's design for humanity. We build strong relationships with our students, colleagues, and leaders. We are creating a more connected community and world. Through our relationships, we are doing life-changing, society-shifting work.

Today's Intention:

_____

_____

_____

_____

May the Lord Bless You and Keep You:

Today, may you feel wholeheartedly connected to those around you.
May you feel the close relationship between you and Jesus.
May the Holy Spirit guide you in forming a strong, trusting community with others.
And may your place of work and community be more interconnected because of your example.

Memorable Moment:

_____

_____

_____

_____

I AM SOMEBODY

"I gave my students a saying to say: 'I am somebody.
I was somebody when I came,
I'll be a better somebody when I leave.
I am powerful, and I am strong.
I deserve the education that I get here."
~ Rita Pierson [11]

In our reflections together, we often consider our students and those around us. This is important because we are called to be in service to others. However, today I would like to start with you.

Do you feel like *somebody* today? When you step into your workspace, are you treated as *somebody?* I hope and pray the answer is, "yes," with examples of encouragement and validation coming to your mind, but I know this may not be a reality for you at this time.

Just so you hear it from someone today: You are incredibly important. There has never been a YOU before, and there never will be again. God designed you exactly as you are. In you, He instilled strengths, dreams, passion, joy, and identity. You are an essential part of God's plan for His Kingdom. The way others treat you, whether intentionally or subconsciously, in no way measures your worth. You are His workmanship, created in Christ Jesus. It is through Christ's lens that we are able to view ourselves with full acceptance, embracing His sacrifice for us. Our focus is no longer on our sin or brokenness, but on what Jesus is doing in and through our lives.

Now let's focus on those around us. How powerful would it be if, regardless of how we are viewed or treated, we chose to treat everybody like a *somebody*. No matter what. Period. God created our students and colleagues, and they bear His image. They deserve dignity and appreciation of their humanity. Be the powerful spark that ignites a shifting atmosphere all around you.

Today's Intention:

_____

_____

_____

_____

May the Lord Bless You and Keep You:

May you know you are a somebody today.
You are God's somebody, and you are called to a great purpose.
May your presence, words, and actions uplift those around you.
May your building become a holy space where people belong, have a voice, and are uplifted.

Memorable Moment:

_____

_____

_____

_____

I AM PURSUED

"What do you think? If a man owns a hundred sheep, and one of them wanders away, will he not leave the ninety-nine on the hills and go look for the one that wandered off? And if he finds it, truly I tell you, he is happier about that one sheep than about the ninety-nine that did not wander off. In the same way your Father in heaven is not willing that any of these little ones should perish."
~ Matthew 18:12-14 (NIV)

Think of that *one* student. (You know the one I'm talking about.) Or perhaps there are about twenty in your situation. They are the ones who need more energy and love than you feel like you have to give. They are the ones you cry and pray over during your prep time. They are the students who have literally or figuratively torn your classroom apart because they are hurting. From this hurt we are left thinking, *I don't deserve this* and at the same time, *I'm not doing enough.*

Day after day, we do our best to try new approaches, develop new plans, and prepare ourselves and the rest of the class for whatever new "adventure" that day may bring. But it's heartbreaking and exhausting. We may feel lost, ill-equipped, and incredibly alone. We can probably relate to the shepherd in Jesus' story. I cannot tell you how many times I have had to leave "the ninety-nine" to literally look for the one who wandered off!

However, here is a truth to take with us today: we are both *shepherd* and *sheep*. We need shepherding just like our students do. Jesus, our Good Shepherd, has already gone before us to pursue us and our students. We are not going alone. He does not give up on any of us, and by His Spirit, we will not give up on our pursuit either.

Today's Intention:

_____

_____

_____

_____

May the Lord Bless You and Keep You:
Today, you are searched for and pursued by Jesus.
He desperately wants to create a deeper relationship with you.
May you have the wisdom, grace, and strength to continue pursuing
your students.
May new doors open and trusting relationships be built.
And may you never give up doing all you can to find the lost.

Memorable Moment:

_____

_____

_____

_____

I AM LOYAL

"Love bears all things, believes all things, hopes all things, endures all things."
~ 1 Corinthians 13:7 (ESV)

Our reflection verse for today is often heard at weddings. We think of a couple so connected to each other, they commit to bear, believe, hope, and endure all things together. Through strong seasons and challenging times, they choose to be loyal and begin the next day in love.

Loyalty means to give or show firm, constant support to a person or thing. Rather than simply a feel-good sentiment, loyalty invokes a sense of power and determination: a firm display of constant support. Our reflection verse from 1 Corinthians is a definition of loyalty. Paul's words describe loving unconditionally, trusting others' lived experiences, and never ceasing to hope for better things. Loyalty is enduring all things for the sake of the one with whom you are loyal.

We are called to be loyal to our students, showing firm and constant support. This commitment is the backbone of our advocacy and belief as teachers. We create a space where boundaries are established and respected, and where trust is cultivated. On positive days and difficult days, we bear, believe, hope, and endure all things, grounded in the matchless love of Christ. This support goes deeper still. How are we talking about our students when they are not around? How are we consistently demonstrating support and advocacy? The answers to these questions are powerful.

Today's Intention:

_____

_____

_____

_____

May the Lord Bless You and Keep You:

Today, may you feel the firm and constant support of your loyal Father.
May you be given a new directive to be uncommonly loyal to others.
May your faith and loyalty be grounded in the love of Christ.
May you fiercely believe that God has a purpose for all people.
May your students sense your loyalty and devotion to them.
And may God use your trust and obedience to bless your space of learning.

Memorable Moment:

_____

_____

_____

_____

I AM UNCONDITIONAL

**"When people show you who they are,
believe them the first time."
~ Maya Angelou** [12]

To be unconditional means to be without conditions. Do you think our spaces of learning are designed to be unconditional? Why or why not? Do you believe these environments should be unconditional?

Maybe the conversation shifts slightly, or significantly, when we specify: unconditional love. Although it is challenging to comprehend at times, I know Jesus loves me without conditions. Rooted in this truth, I believe it is a crucial part of my calling to unconditionally love those around me. However, this is *much* easier said than done.

I will be real with you. Maya Angelou's quote makes me feel a little uncomfortable. (That's probably why I included it in our reflection today.) The idea of wholeheartedly believing someone and unconditionally loving them for exactly how they show up in the moment feels vulnerable or naive. My mind races to remind me that we need expectations, boundaries, and accountability. Yes, all of that is true, but let us return our gaze to our Father. He has expectations, boundaries, and accountability for us as His children, and yet His love is so powerful and matchless that He also loves us exactly as we are in this moment. Nothing we can do will ever change this. When we dwell on His example of love for us, we are given the freedom to pursue a deeper understanding of unconditional love for those around us.

Today's Intention:

_____

_____

_____

_____

May the Lord Bless You and Keep You:

Today, may you be drawn to unconditionally love yourself and others.
May your heart be convicted of those you have felt content to disregard.
Through His life, death, and resurrection, may Christ grow your capacity to love those around you.
May you find freedom in choosing love over hate or dismissal.
And may your awareness of Christ's love for you deepen beyond measure.

Memorable Moment:

_____

_____

_____

_____

I AM SEARCHING

**"You will seek me and find me
when you seek me with all your heart."
~ Jeremiah 29:13 (NIV)**

What are you searching for today?

Do you find yourself searching for answers, time, energy, financial opportunities, breakthroughs in your mental or physical health, or restoration in your family and relationships?

Perhaps, you feel beyond the point of searching and are now just focused on doing the next thing in front of you. Sometimes just the mindset of researching, making decisions, and trying to find answers can feel overwhelming all on its own. If you are reflecting in this space today, exhausted from searching and fixing, know that you are not alone.

I wonder what the underlying purpose of our searching is. Are we hoping to find peace, safety, or a sense of belonging? When we cut right to the source of our longing, we will most likely find ourselves at the foot of the cross, desperately seeking what Jesus is ready to provide. But when we believe *our* answers and extra hard work will suffice, we may lose out on a bigger picture that God sees. Ultimately, our true peace, security, and belonging can only be found in Christ. When we seek Him first, everything else has a way of working itself out.

Today's Intention:

_____

_____

_____

_____

May the Lord Bless You and Keep You:
Today, may the Holy Spirit calm your anxious heart.
May your endless tasks feel less important than your relationship with Jesus.
May searching for answers shift to searching for Christ in your
daily activities.
In seeking Him, may you find peace, comfort, and love.
And may this peace be contagious to all those in your midst.

Memorable Moment:

_____

_____

_____

_____

I AM A PEACEMAKER

"You're blessed when you can show people how to cooperate instead of compete or fight. That's when you discover who you really are, and your place in God's family."
~ Matthew 5:9 (MSG)

Some passages of Scripture feel like they were written just for those who work in education or have a role in raising up the next generation. These verses are relatable and applicable at this very moment. Our reflection verse today is one of those for me.

When was the last time you showed people how to cooperate, instead of how to compete or fight? Yesterday? A week ago? A month ago? Five minutes ago? In the midst of lesson planning, data tracking, ongoing communication, and so many more tasks which fill our days, coaching into cooperation may seem so natural that it doesn't initially come to mind.

How personal it is that Jesus took the time to identify this action and *bless* it! He sees you. Perhaps, your goal is to finally finish that one lesson without an interruption or outburst. But once again, you are asked to intervene for a student who is having a tough day. Even though you know there are underlying reasons behind the behavior, this situation is draining on you as the peacemaker and exhausting for the student. Regardless, you step in, protect, and coach. You pray for the capacity to love unconditionally. Our Loving Savior sees the feelings you may hide from others, and He blesses you for your peaceful intercession.

Today's Intention:

_____

_____

_____

_____

May the Lord Bless You and Keep You:

Today, may you be given renewed grace once again.
As you step into a new day, unsure of what it will bring, may you feel
deep Peace, knowing God goes with you.
In the times you are called to be a peacemaker, may you feel
intimately blessed.
As days continue, may you begin to see evidence of your love and
determination in those around you.

Memorable Moment:

_____

_____

_____

_____

I AM A MEDIATOR

"We are made to exist in a delicate network of interdependence. We are sisters and brothers, whether we like it or not. To treat anyone as if they were less than human, less than a brother or a sister, no matter what they have done, is to contravene the very laws of our humanity. And those who shred the web of interconnectedness cannot escape the consequences of their actions."
~ Desmond Tutu & Mpho Tutu [13]

This quote by Desmond Tutu feels powerful to me. Take a moment to read it again through the lens of our communities, society, and world.

Now, read our quote one more time through the lens of your learning space. Some of our students' life experiences have been so divisive that unity and understanding are foreign concepts. Perhaps today, these feel like foreign concepts to you as well. I have been there. It feels uncomfortable to be divided. Something within me feels physically unsettled when I allow myself to treat someone as if they were less than human. When this happens, God shows up as my Mediator. Because He created all of us in His image, He is the link that connects us together.

We are put in positions of enormous possibility for positive impact. We may not be able to alter society's perceptions of one another, but the way we cultivate a community within our classrooms can change *everything* for the learners present in that space. By Christ's example, we are the connectors, the bridge-builders, the mediators.

Today's Intention:

_____

_____

_____

_____

May the Lord Bless You and Keep You:

Today, may you find opportunities to create and mediate connections.
On days when hope seems to fade, may God remind you once again of our connection to each other.
May you not be distracted by voices that would have you believe someone is unworthy of belonging.
Instead, may you feel renewed by the interconnected design of our world.

Memorable Moment:

_____

_____

_____

_____

I AM AN ADVOCATE

"The ultimate measure of a man is not where he stands in moments of comfort and convenience, but where he stands at times of challenge and controversy."
~ Dr. Martin Luther King, Jr. [14]

The word, "advocate," is used several times in the New Testament to describe either the Holy Spirit or Jesus. Originally, this word was written in Greek as, "parakletos." Parakletos can be translated as either "advocate" or "comforter." Someone who is described in this way pleads another's cause, helping them by defending or comforting.

Have you ever felt targeted or under attack? Working with students, families, and communities, we may feel extremely scrutinized or be at the receiving end of accusation. In these moments, do you feel supported and advocated for? Whether your answer is yes or no, take a moment to reflect on how this feels.

Now, I invite you to breathe in a powerful breath as you read these next words: Jesus Christ - through whom God defeated death and who loves you unconditionally - is *your* Advocate. You are not on trial in front of Him. He takes the stand *for* you. And because the Holy Spirit lives within you, you are empowered to be an advocate for others as well. Look around your space of Holy learning today. Do your students feel targeted or under attack? Perhaps God has called you to be here for such a time as this to defend and comfort them.

Today's Intention:

_____

_____

_____

_____

May the Lord Bless You and Keep You:

May you take strong steps today, confident in God's undefeated advocacy. When the enemy seems to be closing in with accusations and shame, may you boldly proclaim Jesus Christ is with you and standing for you. May you have eyes to see the hurt and the needs around you. Empowered by the Holy Spirit, may you have the courage to stand up and speak up for those treated unjustly.

Memorable Moment:

_____

_____

_____

_____

I AM THOUGHTFUL

**"You're blessed when you get your inside world - your mind
and heart - put right. Then you can see God in the outside
world."**
~ Matthew 5:8 (MSG)

A couple of years into my teaching career, I first learned about
the word: "metacognition." If you need a refresher,
metacognition means thinking about your thinking. I like to use
this word with students to model how we can reflect as we are
learning new content. It's a pretty abstract concept at first, but
the more we continually use this word in practice, the more
students' understanding grows into application.

What is your own personal metacognitive status? Do you think
about your own thinking? Throughout your day, are your
thoughts mostly positive, negative, or somewhere in the middle?
How about stressful, hurried, or chaotic? Some of you may be
wondering, *who has the time to think about their thinking?*

It can feel overwhelming to pause and reflect on our thoughts,
but there is significant value in recognizing our brain's behavior.
In our verse for today, Jesus invites us to consider the activity of
our minds and hearts. When we understand our thoughts,
feelings, and emotions, we can interact with the world around us
in a more productive and positive way. If this feels
uncomfortable, you are not alone. Start small by just being aware
of your thoughts today. You may be surprised by what you
notice.

Today's Intention:

_____

_____

_____

_____

May the Lord Bless You and Keep You:

Today, may you feel compelled to be thoughtful.
May you allow yourself space and grace to reflect on your mind and heart.
May you notice the beautiful colors of your soul.
May the Holy Spirit show you areas where you may be experiencing unhealthy thought patterns.
And may your thoughtfulness spark an awareness into God's perspective of the world.

Memorable Moment:

_____

_____

_____

_____

I AM HUMBLE

"Therefore, as God's chosen people, holy and dearly loved, clothe yourselves with compassion, kindness, humility, gentleness, and patience."
~ Colossians 3:12 (NIV)

Humility is gracious,

Offering thanks for daily acts of consideration.

Humility is focused,

Staying in one's own lane instead of merging into oncoming traffic.

Humility is reflective,

Acknowledging opportunities given and help generously provided.

Humility is forgiving,

Recognizing no one is free from error and all deserve fresh

opportunities.

Humility is selfless,

Considering others' experiences and areas of need.

Humility is Christ,

Taking on the responsibilities of a servant to show love to the world.

Today's Intention:

_____

_____

_____

_____

May the Lord Bless You and Keep You:

May the Holy Spirit develop authentic humility in you.
May you be in tune with God and those around you, recognizing the
needs of others.
May you feel continually thankful for all the blessings given to you.
May you remain centered in your calling, giving all the glory to God.

Memorable Moment:

_____

_____

_____

_____

I AM CONSISTENT

"Therefore, my dear brothers and sisters, stand firm. Let nothing move you. Always give yourselves fully to the work of the Lord, because you know that your labor in the Lord is not in vain."
~ 1 Corinthians 15:58 (NIV)

In my opinion, one of the most impactful characteristics of a quality educator is consistency. Trustworthiness is developed when one is consistent in their personal and professional work habits. Students find comfort and security in a space in which expectations, procedures, and consequences are dependable. Of course, life happens and not every day can be perfectly planned and executed. However, it is immeasurably valuable when students can anticipate what their day will look like, how a teacher will respond, and what they are expected to do.

Consider how you feel when you are around someone who is consistent. Perhaps a family member, colleague, or professional leader comes to mind. How do you feel when this person is committed to a task, consistent in communication, and not shaken easily? Do you demonstrate these qualities with others?

It may look different for each of us, but I believe God instructs us to be consistent in our actions, both personally and professionally. In our reflection verse, Paul reminds us to stand firm and let nothing be able to move us. When we commit ourselves to developing consistency in our lives, this brings honor to God. Others notice. They witness our work ethic, integrity, and focus, ultimately bringing the glory back to God.

Today's Intention:

_____

_____

_____

_____

May the Lord Bless You and Keep You:

Today, may you reflect on your consistency.
May you show respect to others by being true to your word.
May you be efficient with your time, so you can accomplish what needs to be done.
May the Holy Spirit strengthen you to show consistency in your attitude and demeanor.
And may God give you grace for the disruptions and challenges that will enter your day.

Memorable Moment:

_____

_____

_____

_____

I AM A PLANTER

**"Though you can easily count the seeds in an apple,
it's impossible to count the apples in a seed."
~ Proverb [15]**

For a moment, imagine a gardener planning their upcoming field. The gardener has selected the types of vegetables, fruit, and flowers they want to grow. These are their goals. They have done research on the appropriate soil, nutrients, water amount, and sunlight each type of seed will need to grow successfully. They cultivate the ground. They carefully place each seed or bulb where it should go. Then, the gardener waits and trusts. They know they will have to be patient for some time in order to see the impact of their labor.

As teachers, we are familiar with intentional planning, research into best practices, and cultivating spaces for growth to take place. The reality of waiting and trusting for growth is often more taxing than we realize. We rarely see the outcomes of our efforts quickly. Yes, this is a part of the job, but it can be disheartening nonetheless.

My simple encouragement for you today is to not count on growth happening exactly when you want it to. It *will* happen. I firmly believe this. God has called you to *this space* for *this season* with *these students* for a divine purpose. He is using your impact to shape the lives of every learner in your midst. You may not see it yet, but trust God's purpose and plan. And keep planting.

Today's Intention:

_____

_____

_____

_____

May the Lord Bless You and Keep You:

Today, may you enter your place of teaching as a divine planter.
May you offer encouraging words, sowing seeds of hope.
May you feel an overwhelming peace from God, knowing you are making a difference.
And may God abundantly bless you with glimpses of sprouts and buds along your journey.

Memorable Moment:

_____

_____

_____

_____

I AM A STORYTELLER

**"Owning our story and loving ourselves through that process
is the bravest thing we'll ever do."
~ Brené Brown [16]**

I believe (and several research studies back me up on this) stories are one of the most powerful ways to engage an audience. During my first year of teaching, I taught a group of wonderful students, but there was no doubt that engagement had been an ongoing challenge. It didn't help that for the first two months of the school year, there were a few students who consistently mimicked barnyard animal noises while instruction was taking place. While at times I recognized how truly amusing this was, it was exhausting to think of new ideas for positive behavior reinforcement and rational, clear-cut consequences.

I still remember the first time I sat the entire class down on the rug and told them a personal, real-talk story. I couldn't believe it! Every single student was silently listening the entire time. This was a breakthrough for our class. From then on, as I developed lesson plans, I thought of captivating stories that would connect with our learning objectives. It took some practice. As we all know, there are *good* storytellers who hold our attention in the palm of their hands, and there are those whose storytelling skills are in progress.

Truthfully, I'm still working on developing in this area. However, a lack of experience or comfortability should not stop me from listening to and sharing stories. Jesus used parables as a key method of teaching. He chose relatable topics and simple examples. Stories connect us together, and when we feel connected and seen, it becomes so much easier for our brains to engage in comprehending and retaining additional information.

Today's Intention:

_____

_____

_____

_____

May the Lord Bless You and Keep You:

Today, may stories fill your mind and ignite your spirit.
May you be reminded of stories recorded in the Bible, building up your faith.
May you listen to others, validating their experiences.
And may you be inspired to grow your storytelling skills to invite connection with those around you.

Memorable Moment:

_____

_____

_____

_____

I AM A READER

"We read to know we're not alone."
~ William Nicholson [17]

As professionals working in the education system, many of us would likely consider ourselves as readers. We have read a lot to get to this point. Perhaps the enjoyment of reading is a hobby or helps relieve stress. If I was sitting next to you today, I would love to hear your answers to these questions:

Do you enjoy reading fiction or nonfiction books?
Who are some of your favorite authors?
Do you have an all-time favorite book?
Do you have a "reading spot"? If so, describe it.

For a long time, I did not consider myself an avid reader. As a child, I made expected progress in my reading skills, and I completed required assignments, but I never found enjoyment in this practice. Then in college, a professor told us something that completely shifted my perspective. To summarize, she emphasized reading is the most important area to model and teach effectively because, with this knowledge, someone can open a Bible and understand for themself the saving grace of the Gospel. Woah! I had never thought about this before. Modeling my love of reading and empowering the next generation to be skilled, confident readers means there are no limits to what my students can explore about God and the world around them.

I am happy to report that I now consider myself a reader. As for me, I love nonfiction books. I seek out authors who will challenge my mindset and habits. One of my all-time favorites is a hidden-treasure picture book called, "The Big Orange Splot," by Daniel Pinkwater.[18] And I love reading next to the fireplace.

Today's Intention:

_____

_____

_____

_____

May the Lord Bless You and Keep You:

Today, may you be reminded of the privilege it is to read and have access to new knowledge.

May you be inspired to share your love of reading with those around you.

May you find a wonderful new book to entertain you, shift your perspective, or comfort you.

May your passion for reading plant seeds, growing into others' exploration of God and His creation.

Memorable Moment:

_____

_____

_____

_____

I AM A DEVELOPER

"The function of education is to teach one to think intensively and to think critically. Intelligence plus character - that is the goal of true education."
~ Dr. Martin Luther King Jr. [19]

A crucial aspect of our calling is supporting development. Individuals working with children and youth are experts in the areas of social-emotional, physical, and cognitive development. In collaborative discussions, we often analyze whether or not students are meeting targeted developmental milestones. All throughout the school year, we work with students, intentionally promoting growth in these domains.

However, we know our role as developer stretches far beyond state and national academic standards. We have the honor of creating opportunities for students to think intensively and critically. When we support the upcoming generation in building these skills, what a difference that will make for our communities and world! This type of development is deep and powerful.

Consider how the Holy Spirit has been developing you to think intensively and critically. Rooted in our faith, we grow in our ability to view the world from God's perspective: to see the needs He sees. To hear the cries He hears. To form solutions based on empathy and understanding with a long-term impact. Perhaps, *that is the goal of true education.*

Today's Intention:

_____

_____

_____

_____

May the Lord Bless You and Keep You:
Today, may you reflect on the areas God has been working on and developing in you.
May God place people and situations in your life, continuing to shape you.
May your passion for developing others grow.
May the Holy Spirit give you wisdom and understanding in building opportunities for development.

Memorable Moment:

_____

_____

_____

_____

I AM FLEXIBLE

**"Progress is impossible without change,
and those who cannot change their minds cannot change
anything."
~ George Bernard Shaw** [20]

The ability to think flexibly is one of the most underrated skills we possess. Have you ever observed someone deliver a presentation when a student or audience member shifted the entire dialogue? An experienced speaker is able to navigate this unexpected route and still meet the intended outcome. It is inspiring to watch! The room immediately feels more engaged because this authentic learning opportunity was welcomed.

When I invite flexible instructional approaches into my practice, I am more relaxed and in the moment, comfortable with the content and audience I am teaching. Welcoming students' ideas and choices into the learning space guides where we take our learning. It feels alive and freeing! It takes the pressure off of my "perfectly planned lesson" and allows me to embrace new approaches in the moment.

In his quote, George Bernard Shaw emphasizes the importance of thinking flexibly about the world around us. As we discussed earlier, it is essential to be proactive and well-planned. However, to create a space for all voices to be included, whether in staff meetings or in classrooms, we need to reflect on our mindset. Are we stuck on what we *need* to have happen or how a lesson has *always* been taught? Or can we risk letting go just a bit in order to be open to new perspectives and learning opportunities?

Today's Intention:

_____

_____

_____

_____

May the Lord Bless You and Keep You:

*Today, may you be given a surprising sense of freedom.
May you be grounded in the unshakable areas of your faith and calling.
May you think flexibly and creatively, following the Holy Spirit's movement in your life.
May you have ears to hear the voices and experiences of those around you.
By opening your hands and trusting God with your day, may you feel burdens lifted.*

Memorable Moment:

_____

_____

_____

_____

I AM AN ENCOURAGER

"So speak encouraging words to one another. Build up hope so you'll all be together in this, no one left out, no one left behind."
~ 1 Thessalonians 5:11 (MSG)

What is your favorite part about working in education? What do you find the most rewarding?

For me, having an opportunity to encourage others is one of my favorite parts about teaching. Whether I am interacting with my students, my colleagues, or those in leadership, I enjoy the chance to build others up. I suppose this can be true of any profession; however, the role of an educator is unique in that we have, seemingly endless opportunities every day to make a lasting impact through our words and actions.

Even though encouraging others is important to me, I have found, the further I journey into the school year, the less encouragement I give. I am not entirely certain why this happens. Perhaps, as the year gets busier and more overwhelming, I start to let go of the pieces of teaching that I love the most: uplifting others and offering encouraging words and actions. Thankfully, I've begun to recognize when these practices begin to fade. Then I have time to intervene and intentionally incorporate authentic encouragement when I am working and learning.

Think about the last few days. What did you say or do that may have had a positive, lasting impact for a student? We may never truly know what will resonate, and I think that's okay. However, we can imagine what words or actions may be perspective-altering. We can seize opportunities to identify strengths in others. Let's decide together right now: what might your students take away from your impact in the coming days and weeks?

Today's Intention:

_____

_____

_____

_____

May the Lord Bless You and Keep You:

Today, may you be blessed to be a blessing to others.
May you seek opportunities to authentically encourage those around you.
In every word of encouragement you give, may your heart also feel uplifted.
And may God use your encouragement now to create a lifelong impact.

Memorable Moment:

_____

_____

_____

_____

I AM AFFECTIONATE

"The conclusion is always the same: love is the most powerful and still the most unknown energy of the world."
~ Pierre Teilhard de Chardin [21]

"Affectionate" may not be a characteristic we quickly associate with our roles in education; however, after looking closer at the definition, we find that it relates well to the work we do. According to *Oxford Languages*, affectionate means: "readily feeling or showing fondness or tenderness."[22] The word, "readily," stands out to me in this definition. This type of kindness is not a gradual development. It is an immediate show of care to another person, without hesitation, questioning, or preconceived judgments.

Consider the various situations we encounter in our school day which require us to readily show fondness or tenderness. We apply a Band-aid on a papercut, even if it isn't gushing blood. Whether or not we have the time built into our schedule, we listen and validate the same stories over and over again. We navigate peer relationships as a mediator, coaching into empathy-building and problem-solving strategies. We provide meaningful academic feedback that creates opportunities for future discoveries. We make ourselves available for students to share personal or school-related concerns. And we welcome new students into our learning spaces on a daily basis.

Let's think more about welcoming that new student. The classroom routines are already established, and your community is strengthening. Perhaps you get a few days or a few hours' notice of your new student's arrival. You know relatively nothing about this individual. Despite all these things, the moment you meet your new student, a warm smile grows on your face, you make direct eye contact, greet the student by name, and graciously introduce yourself. You may ask a question or two and even introduce them to a peer who can help answer their questions. This is affection. You are readily showing a type of unconditional love that sets the course for how this student views themself when they are with you. This is incredibly powerful, creating an atmosphere of safety and belonging in your classroom.

Today's Intention:

_____

_____

_____

_____

May the Lord Bless You and Keep You:

*Today, may you display genuine fondness and tenderness towards
those around you.*
*May your students always know you love what you do when you are
with them.*
May your encouragement bring out the unique gifts in others.
*And may the Holy Spirit give you strength to continue to show love
even in difficult times.*

Memorable Moment:

_____

_____

_____

_____

I AM WOUNDED

"The Lord helps the fallen and lifts those bent beneath their loads."
~ Psalm 145:14 (NLT)

I came home after finishing a day of student teaching. Some of my students were going through extremely challenging life experiences, and I was feeling it with them. I remember crying in the bathtub that night - still such a new teacher. I called my sister who had been a teacher for ten years. I didn't tell her anything about my students or my day. I simply asked, "How do you make it not hurt so much?" I will never forget her response.

With empathy, she replied, "You don't. You will have some days when you feel so joyful. And you will have some days when it hurts so much you can barely take it. But I know I would rather *keep feeling* than come home from work and feel nothing. Because when you choose to not feel the tough things, you miss out on the joyful moments, too."

My friend, today I want you to hear that it is okay to admit we have been wounded by witnessing and supporting students in their difficult circumstances. In our calling, we develop a practical mindset and sometimes a thick skin. Yes, in our daily responsibilities, we need to be calm, keep our emotions in check, and do the next thing. However, if we neglect to recognize the parts of our lives when we have known hurt and trauma through someone else's lived experiences or our own, the pain does not go away. Instead, the thick skin transforms into numbness or anger. When we come before God and acknowledge the ongoing weariness and pain that comes with choosing empathy for others, it does not make us weak. We invite Him into our woundedness, and He reaches out His hand to meet ours. We can rest in the truth that the same strong hand reaches to our students, colleagues, families, and leaders.

Today's Intention:

_____

_____

_____

_____

May the Lord Bless You and Keep You:

When you feel wounded, may you also feel surrounded by grace.
May you allow yourself to sit in the moment and feel.
May this time connect you to the One who intimately knows how you feel.
As you allow space for your own pain to be seen, may this create deeper empathy within you.
And may you have the courage to continue feeling, listening, and loving.

Memorable Moment:

_____

_____

_____

_____

I AM SURRENDERED

"Jesus spoke of freedom, but he spoke of a different kind of freedom: the type of freedom that comes not through power but through submission. Not through control but through surrender."
~ Max Lucado [23]

Join me on this thought process today and see if you can relate. You are overwhelmed when you arrive at work and exhausted when the day is over. You think to yourself, *I can't keep this up for much longer. I need a game plan.* Before you know it, you're deciding to go to work a little earlier each day, and you take a couple of extra tasks home each night, just to keep your head above water. *Just for this week,* you tell yourself.

However, the week is over and you feel more drained and irritable than before. Most likely, there are still items on the to-do list and not enough time to complete them. You're still sinking, but feeling heavier now.

At times, we convince ourselves if we grab onto more control, we will find more freedom and breathing room. But Max Lucado reminds us that freedom often finds us when we begin to let go of control. This does not excuse us from working hard or brainstorming solutions to problems. It means stepping back and reality-checking our expectations. Unfortunately, ours is a profession of many different responsibilities. We simply cannot do it all. So we pray for the discernment to prioritize. We do the next right thing and surrender the rest to God.

Today's Intention:

_____

_____

_____

_____

May the Lord Bless You and Keep You:

Today, may you begin with a renewed sense of peace and freedom.
May your hands relax and open to surrender the things you have held onto so tightly.
May the Holy Spirit give you wisdom to identify and prioritize what is the most important.
May you rest in Jesus' strong arms, knowing He is Sovereign over all.

Memorable Moment:

_____

_____

_____

_____

I AM REDEEMED

"Israel, put your hope in the Lord, for with the Lord is unfailing love and with him is full redemption."
~ Psalm 130:7 (NIV)

"Redemption" is a word we read often in the Bible and hear in our church experiences. Perhaps it becomes one of those words that, without intention, begins to lose its potency. Redemption means being saved from our sin and shortcomings.

Consider how often we carry around our mistakes like bricks in a backpack. We replay every interaction, conversation, and reaction we made throughout the day, wondering if we should have - or could have - handled a situation differently. We may recognize we need to move on and try to ignore these persisting, agonizing thoughts, but for many of us, they build up into a weight too overwhelming to carry. We begin to break under the pressure.

Unfailing love. Full redemption.

Jesus loves you so much. He does not want you to live a life under crushing guilt or resentment. I don't believe God has designed you to live in past experiences. His work is in the here and now. Mistakes do not need to hold power over you because Jesus gave His life to bring you freedom in your life. He forgives you even before you are able to forgive yourself. I pray this reality sinks in deeply for you today, and you will find openness and safety in His unfailing love and grace.

Today's Intention:

_____

_____

_____

_____

May the Lord Bless You and Keep You:

Today, may you find a quiet moment to come before your Savior.
Come as you are: messy, tired, grateful, reflective, or regretful.
May His unfailing love break through the lies that guilt and shame
want you to believe.
Nothing you do could ever separate you from God's love, grace, and
redemption.
May you be given the freedom and strength to forgive yourself,
knowing Christ has already forgiven you.

Memorable Moment:

_____

_____

_____

_____

I AM SHAKEN

"Right now I [Jesus] am shaken. And what am I going to say? 'Father, get me out of this?' No, this is why I came in the first place. I'll say, 'Father, put your glory on display."
~ John 12:27-28 (MSG)

The theme for this reflection, I do not take lightly. To feel shaken is to have lost a sense of control, to be overwhelmed by anxiety, and to feel your innermost being at risk. I pray most of us have never felt these things; however, we know this is a reality for many. Moments when we are shaken to our core can be amplified by the feeling of loneliness. How can anyone understand what we have experienced? Or perhaps, we don't want others to understand. Why share the mess of pain and confusion?

Our reflection verses from the Gospel of John center on an incredibly intimate moment in Jesus' life. He is desperately praying to His Father. He knows in a few short hours He will be arrested, abused, tortured, and killed. *He is shaken.* He doesn't want to be by Himself, so He asks his disciples to stay awake with Him, but they continue to fall asleep. He is alone.

Jesus became fully human, embracing the emotions and circumstances we experience, to demonstrate the extravagant measure of God's love for us. Our Savior understands our loneliness, and He desires to be deeply connected with us in our moments of joy and excitement or pain and grief. If you feel shaken or alone today, my prayer is that you would feel embraced by the comforting love of Jesus as He sits with you, listens, and knows.

Today's Intention:

_____

_____

_____

_____

May the Lord Bless You and Keep You:

In the midst of your experiences: past, present, and future, may you be reminded that Jesus knows you more intimately than you will ever comprehend.
Deeper still, He loves you unconditionally.
May the Holy Spirit comfort you with the unfailing promise that you are never alone.
By Jesus' example, may you seek to put your Father's glory on display.

Memorable Moment:

_____

_____

_____

_____

I AM DRAINED

"Come to me, all you who are weary and burdened, and I will give you rest. Take my yoke upon you and learn from me, for I am gentle and humble in heart, and you will find rest for your souls.
~ Matthew 11:28-29 (NIV)

It was not even ten minutes after I returned from taking my students out to the buses, and I was already writing my to-do list on the whiteboard for that evening. All the while, I was mentally revisiting conversations and interactions I had with students throughout the day. End-of-the-day exhaustion, intertwined with self-criticism and the daily tasks that never end, left me feeling heavy and drained.

Then I received a text from a friend, checking in on my day. In my reply message, I honestly admitted I was tired. The next text was simply: "Matthew 11:28-29. You should look it up right now." I followed the advice. These verses were familiar to me, but something about that moment made me realize that this Scripture passage needed to become my "after school verses."

Perhaps, we need this reminder daily because our responsibilities are overwhelming and our work is incredibly important. God has called us to this profession knowing we cannot do it alone. He must bear the burdens. He invites us to rest and put aside what is outside of our control. Our role is not easy, but we know His mighty hands are stronger than our heaviest burdens.

Today's Intention:

_____

_____

_____

_____

May the Lord Bless You and Keep You:

In the morning, may you come before Christ and entrust the day to Him.
As burdens accumulate in the midst of your day, may your natural reaction
be to bring them to God.
At the end of your day, may you be given the strength and peace to leave
your cares with God, trusting Him for timing, provision, and love.

Memorable Moment:

_____

_____

_____

_____

I AM FILLED

"The questions that matter in life are remarkably few, and they are all answered by the words - 'Come unto Me.'"
~ Oswald Chambers [24]

In the never-ending details and ever so delicate balancing act,

In our moments of heartbreak, confusion, and anger,

In the midst of frustration and seemingly dead-end roads,

Perhaps we need a reset, training our souls in a different way.

We hear: *Come unto Me.*

Our minds race with questions, but the Answer quietly invites:

Come unto Me, My weary child. I will give you rest for your soul.

You will know fullness in the midst of fragility.

You will learn from My example and be filled with Life.

And we pause to reflect on our answer to this invitation.

Will we choose fullness of life?

Our last reflection was entitled, "I am Drained," an obvious antonym to our theme for today. However, we are drawing strength from the same life-giving welcome in Matthew 11:28-29. Accepting this invitation, we shift from feeling drained of energy, passion, or hope, to being filled with love and grace. We lay our burdens down and find ourselves filled with what we truly need: the presence of Jesus.

Today's Intention:

_____

_____

_____

_____

May the Lord Bless You and Keep You:
Today, may you be filled with the Holy Spirit.
When you feel drained or filled, may you come closer to your
loving Teacher.
May you trust that He does have the best plans in store for you.
May Jesus provide rest for your weary soul and refresh your spirit,
heightening your awareness of the blessings in your life.

Memorable Moment:

_____

_____

_____

_____

I AM CLEANSED

"But if we are living in the light, as God is in the light, then we have fellowship with each other, and the blood of Jesus, his Son, cleanses us from all sin."
~ 1 John 1:7 (NLT)

I grew up in Minnesota, a state of diverse landscapes with picturesque lakes, rolling hills, and gorgeous autumn colors. Winters in Minnesota are beautiful and brutal, lasting at least six months. Even though it happens every year, the first substantial snowfall of the season always makes me feel like a kid again! Waking up and opening the curtains to see a fresh covering of white on everything in the neighborhood is magical to me.

There is something powerful and spiritual about this image. No matter what was on the brown, cold grass, the snow covers it completely. Through the months of winter, decay may be happening underneath the surface, but with a fresh blanket of snow, this is not the focus of attention anymore. There is an indescribable beauty that changes the desolate post-autumn dreariness into an unrecognizable wonderland.

Those of us who have experienced this joy know it is also accompanied by a crisp, bitter chill in the air. Cleansing is freeing and necessary, but it can also feel uncomfortable at times. Jesus forgives us completely of our mistakes, regrets, and shortcomings. He wipes the slate of our hearts clean, like the snow cleansing the environment around it. However, acknowledging the messy, decaying parts of ourselves requires us to be vulnerable, while desiring to become clean. The question is: do we desire to be seen, loved, and valued for who we are *and* still grow, change, and be cleansed?

Today's Intention:

_____

_____

_____

_____

May the Lord Bless You and Keep You:
You are known and unconditionally loved.
There is not one part of your history that is not known and felt by your loving Father.
May you embrace Christ's grace and abounding presence today.
May you forgive yourself completely, knowing Jesus has already forgiven you.
And may you feel refreshed with new energy, cleansed, and cherished.

Memorable Moment:

_____

_____

_____

_____

I AM A TEAMMATE

"How good and pleasant it is when God's people live together in unity."
~ Psalm 133:1 (NIV)

A vital part of our work, as educators, is collaboration. Perhaps some of you read the title for this reflection and smiled, thinking of the wonderful team you work with. Others may have a less contented reaction. This is a reality no matter where one is employed. The team we are on makes a huge difference in our productivity, effectiveness, and overall health in the workplace. So we can agree with the Psalmist that it is good and pleasant to live together in unity. But, we can also be honest with ourselves: *easier said than done.*

How do we strengthen an already great team culture or shift a challenging one? An impactful practice is to remember what is and is not within your control. What *is* in your control is your mental space and actions. If you remain laser-focused on your calling (your learners) and the actions you can accomplish to progress your team, you can let go of all of the "other stuff" that doesn't need to take up brain space.

What *is not* in your control is your teammates' thoughts and actions. Yes, they impact you; there is no changing that. But no, you do not need to try to change how they operate individually. Instead, simply focus on the attitude and actions you are bringing to the table. It only takes one strong person to begin to shift the entire atmosphere of a space. It could start with you today.

Today's Intention:

_____

_____

_____

_____

May the Lord Bless You and Keep You:

Today, may God give you a new lens in which to view His children.
May you notice the strengths of your teammates.
May you find supernatural patience and peace as you collaborate with those around you.
May you have clarity in decision-making and take positive action steps.
And may you begin by listening and understanding, as Christ has empathized with you.

Memorable Moment:

_____

_____

_____

_____

I AM CONTAGIOUS

"A teacher affects eternity; he can never tell where his influence stops."
~ Henry Adams [25]

Building on our previous reflection, let's explore our "circle of control" today. The circle of control is an idea many researchers and writers have referenced that illustrates what is within our control and what is not. This visual can be helpful. Picture a circle. Inside the circle are your daily choices: your thoughts, attitudes, words, and actions. Anything outside the circle are things you cannot control: other people's decisions, the weather, the traffic, etc.

While I was student teaching, my mentoring teacher continually reminded me to consider my circle of control. Sometimes, in the midst of a chaotic day, we would pause our teaching, glance at each other, and form a circle with our hands. This was a subtle reminder to focus on the actions we had control over, instead of trying to change things we could not. The miracle of this mindset is that our mood, dialogue, and small choices actually do shift the space when we are in a facilitative role. We simply need to focus on keeping ourselves in check and, in the process, others may find comfort and security in these actions as well.

We can be contagious in a really positive way. Our words of encouragement to others, uplifting self-talk, and grace we show to ourselves and those around us, transmit within our environment. Soon, we may notice our students and colleagues becoming more encouraging, confident, and gracious.

Today's Intention:

_____

_____

_____

_____

May the Lord Bless You and Keep You:
Today, may you reflect on what is within your control.
May you prayerfully entrust to God anything outside of your ability to impact or change.
May you be responsible for your actions, attitudes, and words.
And may God use your encouraging spirit to light a spark, leading to positive changes around you.

Memorable Moment:

_____

_____

_____

_____

I AM A FRIEND

"A friend loves at all times, and a brother is born for a time of adversity."
~ Proverbs 17:17 (NIV)

We carry many identities with us in our personal and professional lives. Being a teacher, in and of itself, encompasses more than the 180 themes in this book. All of us hold additional roles outside of our professional responsibilities. We may be parents, grandparents, sons, daughters, partners, siblings, mentors, coaches, volunteers, and friends.

In each of these capacities lie blessings and obligations. Today, let's simply focus on friendship because I believe it is vital in our lives, and it can often be overlooked. I want to recognize and honor that on busy days and in stressful seasons, you are a friend to others. Perhaps you have many close relationships in multiple areas of your life, or you may have a few deep friendships that you cultivate. Authentic friendship is an incredible blessing because we are welcomed into another person's life to experience joy and struggle with them.

However your social life takes form, this is an important part of who you are. God brings people into your life to support you and keep you grounded. Being a friend to others and embracing others' friendship can be one of the most powerful experiences we have in life. May God surround each of us with people who will encourage us to be the best we can be, rooted in faith. In turn, we are blessed when we are a blessing to others.

Today's Intention:

_____

_____

_____

_____

May the Lord Bless You and Keep You:
Today, may you take a moment to reach out to a friend.
May God bless you with encouragement and love from those closest to you.
May your circle strengthen in compassion and connection.
And may God bring new people into your life to offer fresh perspectives.

Memorable Moment:

_____

_____

_____

_____

Part 3
I Am
Courageous

I AM COURAGEOUS

"It's never too late to begin living more courageously."
~ Brendon Burchard [26]

We are stepping into a season of courage, my friend. This can be a difficult time of the year and will require us to grab hold of God's hand, taking each next step in trust. We are reminded that our Heavenly Teacher goes before us, beside us, and behind us, providing hope and strength in our moments of joy or challenge. We journey together, knowing we are never alone.

On days when more courage is required of us, we can be inspired by those who are showing up and living courageously. We are motivated when a student shows bravery: raising their hand for the first time, answering a question incorrectly, standing up for someone else, asking for help, embracing an identity, and vulnerably sharing a difficult circumstance at home. We are empowered when our colleagues teach with tenacity: creating new ideas, taking risks, seeking support, advocating for our students, and honestly reflecting on their experiences. Our students and teammates are walking through challenging seasons as well. When resilience and grit are demonstrated, it is important to notice.

We look to the coming weeks and months, inviting new opportunities and adventures. There will continue to be difficult days as well. Remember: only in the dirt, bathed with refreshing water, will seeds sprout and grow. We will not be defeated in this season, and neither will our students. They are more courageous than we realize, and we also have more potential for strength and stamina than we often admit to ourselves or others. Let us walk together through this time knowing with God, nothing is impossible.

Today's Intention:

_____

_____

_____

_____

May the Lord Bless You and Keep You:

Today, you may be facing difficult and heartbreaking circumstances.
May you know beyond a shadow of a doubt that God has not and will not leave you.
May you see examples of courage all around you.
May you take hold of God's hand in faithful trust, courageously taking steps forward.
And may you embrace a deep confidence that God will carry you through this time.

Memorable Moment:

_____

_____

_____

_____

I AM A PATHFINDER

"You make known to me the path of life; you will fill me with joy in your presence, with eternal pleasures at your right hand."
~ Psalm 16:11 (NIV)

A pathfinder has the courage to go first,

Paving the way for others.

A pathfinder explores new ways to forge ahead,

Clearing debris and clutter.

It is not necessary for a pathfinder to know all of the answers

before beginning,

For they trust their God-given curiosity and innovative skills.

It is not required for a pathfinder to know what will be at the end

of the path they are seeking,

For they trust the Pathfinder who leads them.

A pathfinder is inspired by those who have paved other ways,

Listening to their stories and craving their energy.

A pathfinder is driven to seek new roads for those coming after,

For one of those may create a new path of their own,

Inspiring others to do the same.

Today's Intention:

_____

_____

_____

_____

May the Lord Bless You and Keep You:
Today, you are called to create new paths for your learners.
May you be given wisdom to remove barriers and open doors.
May your heart be discontent with, "good enough," your eyes searching for a new way.
And may the Holy Spirit lead you to the paths God has already forged.

Memorable Moment:

_____

_____

_____

_____

I AM ADVENTUROUS

"Awaken your spirit to adventure;
Hold nothing back, learn to find ease in risk;
Soon you will be home in a new rhythm,
For your soul senses the world that awaits you."
~ John O'Donohue [27]

When people discover I am a teacher, one of the most common questions I receive is: "What is that like? It must be really difficult!" Usually I reply, "It's always an adventure!" And what an adventure it is!

Consider your daily experiences, the statements you never thought you would say, and the situations you never anticipated finding yourself in. As a form of reflection today, consider your "Memorable Adventures." These may be humorous or they may be thoughtful. It is up to you. Feel free to write them down or simply take a walk down Memory Lane.

When have you experienced the most joy with your students?

What were you doing? How long ago did this happen?

What is the most surprising thing you ever heard from a student?

What is the most unexpected thing you ever needed to say at your job?

What is the most adventurous teaching experience you have ever had?

What ideas, lessons, or activities do you want to explore as a teacher?

What *new rhythms* might God be inspiring in your soul?

Today, let's awaken our spirits to adventure!

Today's Intention:

_____

_____

_____

_____

May the Lord Bless You and Keep You:

In the midst of your journey, may you be reminded that teaching is an adventurous calling!
May you find humor in the lighthearted moments of your day.
May the Holy Spirit bring you comfort and confidence as you take risks and try new things.
And may God ignite a spirit of adventure in you as you journey toward the world that awaits you.

Memorable Moment:

_____

_____

_____

_____

I AM STRENGTHENED

"So do not fear, for I am with you; do not be dismayed, for I am your God. I will strengthen you and help you; I will uphold you with my righteous right hand."
~ Isaiah 41:10 (NIV)

How often do we read verses about strength and wish we felt it in our own lives? These verses are empowering and designed to uplift us during even the most devastating times. However, there may be days when we meditate on these Scriptures and vulnerably whisper to God: *But when will I feel it? When will I feel strengthened?*

I wonder if we always feel it when we are strengthened. In other words, do we have to feel strong to be strong? In my own life, I have consistently wrestled with this question. When I was 16 years old, I was diagnosed with type 1 diabetes. I had no idea the amount of strength this disease would require of me. Diabetes currently has no cure and requires constant monitoring in order to be healthy and thriving. After years of living with diabetes, I have discovered sometimes strength shows up when I least expect it. Reflecting on the past decade, I can now identify that I am more capable than I ever thought possible. However, in the moments when I was physically fighting to make it to another day, nothing in me felt strong.

We may not recognize how much strength we possess until we move forward and look back on these seasons in our lives. I believe this unexplainable perseverance is God's work in us. He upholds us when we feel weak and defeated. Rooted in God's faithfulness and love, we take our next steps in trust, confident that as time passes, we will see His strength evidenced in our lives.

Today's Intention:

_____

_____

_____

_____

May the Lord Bless You and Keep You:

You are strong. May you embrace this truth regardless of whether or not this feels true.

May you have a deep confidence that simply by being here today, you are strong.

May the truth of God's continued power and presence in your life encourage your heart.

May you reflect on moments when you displayed more strength than you ever thought possible.

May you courageously believe God will never fail to uphold you with His righteous right hand.

Memorable Moment:

_____

_____

_____

_____

I AM WEARY

**"My flesh and heart may fail,
But God is the strength of my heart and my portion forever."
~ Psalm 73:26 (NIV)**

I heard a story not long ago that I'd like to share with you today.

A father took his young daughter on a special outing - just the two of them. He had many wonderful plans for their day: playing at the park, picking out a new toy at her favorite store, and soaring to the skies at a trampoline park. At their first stop, her father asked if she would like to go down the slide. She excitedly responded, "Yes please!" But after one or two times, without explanation, she crawled into her father's lap, closed her eyes, and rested.

When she woke up, the young child asked if they could still go to the store to pick out a new toy. "Of course," he responded. But once they entered the store, she slowly looked around and said she didn't want anything that day. At the trampoline park, the intended highlight of their day, she held her father's hand and made her way from the front of the park to the back. After a minute or two, she muttered, "I'm tired." She climbed into her father's lap once again, closed her eyes, and rested. While she felt excited to do the activities, by this point it was clear she was beginning to come down with a cold. Despite the day she wanted to have, her body and mind were weary. What she needed on that special outing was her father to hold her safely in his arms while she rested.

Do you ever feel like this child, beginning the day with the best intentions in mind, but overcome by weariness at every turn? We have a loving Father who holds and comforts us while we rest. He loves His children deeply, more than we can comprehend. When our worries feel too heavy for our hearts, He speaks words of promise, untangling the anxieties. We are invited once again to come to Him and find rest in His loving arms.

Today's Intention:

_____

_____

_____

_____

May the Lord Bless You and Keep You:
Today, may the Holy Spirit bring peace for your weary soul.
When your body and mind feel as if they are failing, may you be
reminded that God is the strength of your life.
May you take hold of your Father's hand, lay your head on His
shoulder, and find rest.
And may you allow yourself to slow down and simply take the next
step in trust.

Memorable Moment:

_____

_____

_____

_____

I AM BURDENED

"You are not a burden for having burdens that you are learning to lay down. You are not a failure for not reaching the heights you thought you'd reach by now."
~ Morgan Harper Nichols [28]

Today, I would like to share a mental picture which has impacted my life.

Picking up bricks. How often do we do this? Find a useless brick. Pick it up. Place it in our backpacks. Then we find another and another. As if our lives aren't already heavy enough. As if we are not already worn from walking, let alone carrying. Why do we look for bricks - the conversations, the unmet expectations, the perfectionism, the interactions we just can't let go of? Why do we choose to carry unnecessary weight? Along our way, we could be picking up flowers, the sweet moments God has given to cheer us on. Is it because we see so many others also accumulating bricks on their backs? Is it because we have only trained our eyes to notice bricks instead of flowers?

To make it even more complicated, we often blame ourselves or others for the weight we are carrying. We know there is a better way, but we feel too tired, confused, or stressed to open our backpacks and lift the weight from our shoulders. How do we change this pattern?

We are invited to begin with an honest conversation with our Heavenly Father. *We are not a burden for having burdens we are learning to lay down.* Then, we decide to take the bricks out of the backpack and bring them out into the open, laying them down at the foot of the cross. When our arms are too weak to lift them, we will ask God to help us. He is the only One who can really lift them anyway. Then we find the freedom to turn our eyes to the flowers and pause to smell the roses.

Today's Intention:

_____

_____

_____

_____

May the Lord Bless You and Keep You:

May you have new eyes to recognize the bricks and flowers in your life.
May you become aware of the worries, conversations, and actions you have carried for far too long.
May the Holy Spirit give you the courage to release and lay them down before God.
In these actions of strength and vulnerability, may you find freedom.
Today, may you choose flowers over bricks, and find rest.

Memorable Moment:

_____

_____

_____

_____

I AM PRESENT

**"This is where God meets me, in the hard stuff.
And I am not defined by the hard thing but by the One who
walks me through it."
~ Emily Ley [29]**

Do you ever feel like we compartmentalize God? I resonate with this. In my morning routine, I take time to spend with God, writing an intention for the day and saying a prayer. Then I go about my day, working through my checklist in the classroom and greeting my students when the bell rings. I am soon swept into the fast-paced busyness of a typical teaching day. Often, I am so concerned with being on time and getting the current objective accomplished, when I get home I can barely remember the day from start to finish.

Our ever-present God reminds us to remain in the moment because that is where we will meet Him. In every hurried encounter, additional meeting, and form of communication, Jesus is with us. In every breakthrough for a student, joyful experience with our class, and relationship strengthened, the Holy Spirit is at work. We may forget we are invited to journey with Jesus through the busyness, celebrations, and unexpected adventures. We are not defined by what happened in the day and how we reacted to it. Instead, we find our identity in the One who takes every step with us, for He knows our hearts and understands us completely.

As God is present with us, we are invited to approach life one moment at a time, bringing awareness to our space. Are we present with our students in their questions, stories, and struggles? Do we listen intently to our colleagues as they share their joys and sorrows? Perhaps in the midst of our busy days, these moments are overlooked. However, I sense these seemingly simple experiences are the ones which hold the most importance.

Today's Intention:

_____

_____

_____

_____

May the Lord Bless You and Keep You:
Today, may you be still and reflect on the character of God.
May the Holy Spirit nudge you to pause and be present.
May God feel close to you in your daily activities as you remain in
communication with Him, giving gratitude for your joys and seeking
grace in your trials.
And may your day feel simplified as you focus on the next right thing.

Memorable Moment:

_____

_____

_____

_____

I AM UPLIFTED

"All labor that uplifts humanity has dignity and importance and should be undertaken with painstaking excellence." ~ Dr. Martin Luther King, Jr. [30]

Like many other reflections we have shared, today we explore the beautiful dichotomy between being uplifted and uplifting others. "I am an Uplifter," would have been an appropriate title as well, for certainly we are reaching out to those who are lonely, hurting, and brokenhearted, offering a sense of hope into their lives.

As Dr. King advocated for in our reflection quote, our calling to uplift humanity should not be taken lightly. Rather, it *should be undertaken with painstaking excellence*. Our labor has dignity and importance. Our students and colleagues look to us to provide encouragement and inspiration. This is an honorable, yet sobering responsibility.

For this reason, the main identifier we focus on is that we are uplifted. Ultimately, God does the work of Uplifter, not just for us, but for our students, colleagues, and families. He begins by extending an invitation, equipping us to live out this calling. In His omnipotent wisdom, our gracious Savior knows our stumbling blocks and moments of weakness. Where we may feel unable to encourage or support, Jesus provides grace and strength, continuing to lift us up as we take the next steps, uplifting humanity.

Today's Intention:

_____

_____

_____

_____

May the Lord Bless You and Keep You:
Today, you are uplifted.
May the mental image of being raised up linger in your mind
throughout the day.
May you be empowered to uplift humanity, showing dignity and
treating others with importance.
May the Holy Spirit strengthen you to fulfill your calling with
painstaking excellence.
And may this begin a chain reaction that no force can hinder.

Memorable Moment:

_____

_____

_____

_____

I AM DRIVEN

"Anyone who meets a testing challenge head-on and manages to stick it out is mighty fortunate. For such persons loyally in love with God, the reward is life and more life."
~ James 1:12 (MSG)

One definition of "driven" is to be propelled or motivated by something. This description brings to mind my experiences with stalled vehicles. A mechanism in the car is not functioning the way it should, and as a result, forward movement seems impossible. Then an alternative power source pushes the vehicle, propelling its motion to a location where it can be assessed and tended to, so it can regain the ability to drive.

This year, you have faced many challenges. You have met them head-on because that is what was required of you in the moment. Even though it may not feel like it, you have not given up. You are here. Our days in the classroom may bring utter exhaustion and leave us feeling "stalled." But God, our internal Power Source, propels us forward as we demonstrate perseverance in the tough times. We are transported to places where healing and wholeness are priorities, inviting us to entrust God with our burdens and anxieties.

In this verse from James, we are reminded: by facing challenges with determination and grit, we are given a deeper understanding of life. We may look back on this school year and recognize how these challenges shaped us into people with incredible impact. God leads us into this profession and journeys with us through the difficult, growing times because He knows *the reward is life and more life*. He supplies the energy to show up, advocating for our students and colleagues. We are driven to do our best with what we have been given and allow God's love to drive us forward.

Today's Intention:

_____

_____

_____

_____

May the Lord Bless You and Keep You:

As the morning dawns and a new day awaits, may you be driven and determined to push forward in your calling.
By God's grace, you have demonstrated unbelievable resilience.
Where you feel weak, may the Holy Spirit inspire new life.
Where you feel courageous, may your audacious energy inspire those around you.

Memorable Moment:

_____

_____

_____

_____

I AM BRAVE

"Do not fear what this day, or any day, may bring your way. Concentrate on trusting Me and doing what needs to be done. Relax in My Sovereignty, remembering that I go before you, as well as with you, into each day. Fear no evil, for I can bring good out of every situation you will ever encounter."
~ Sarah Young [31]

Take a moment to picture a scenario displaying bravery. What is happening? Who is involved? Is it ordinary, heroic, rare, or fantastical?

Now, think of a person you know personally who you would describe as brave. What characteristics, attributes, or actions do they show consistently? How do they inspire you or others around them?

Finally, let's do some self-reflection. Would you describe yourself as brave? Why or why not? How have you shown mental or moral strength in the face of danger, fear, or difficulty?

Examples of bravery are all around us. Our reflection quote today reminds us to trust instead of fear. Trusting is incredibly brave. Trusting ourselves, others, and God is perhaps one of the most vulnerable decisions we can make. Bravery is taking another step forward, clinging to the promise a small Baby with a humble beginning brought to us. Reflecting on Jesus' life reminds us of the bravery woven in the choice to love and serve people, exactly as they are. We experience Christ daily as we witness the resilient actions of our colleagues and students. Those we learn and work with every day may be some of the bravest people in the world. This inspiration fuels our own bravery to love unconditionally and trust confidently. The simplest moments of courage are often the strongest.

Today's Intention:

_____

_____

_____

_____

May the Lord Bless You and Keep You:
Today, may you have a new awareness of your bravery.
May you trust God is bringing goodness, hope, and growth out of
every encounter.
May the Holy Spirit give you mental and moral strength when you are
faced with challenges.
May you have eyes to see the bravery around you.
And may God excite your heart to move forward victoriously.

Memorable Moment:

_____

_____

_____

_____

I AM PERSISTENT

"When you get into a tight place and everything goes against you until it seems you cannot hold on a minute longer, never give up then, for that is just the place and time that the tide is turning."
~ Harriet Beecher Stowe [32]

We may recognize the name, Harriet Beecher Stowe, as the author of the anti-slavery novel, *Uncle Tom's Cabin*. Throughout her life, she was committed to advocating for justice and empowering those around her to strive for positive change.

However, until recently I did not know the event which ultimately motivated Harriet to write this book. In 1849, her 18-month-old son died of cholera. Later in life, Stowe revealed that losing her child inspired her to write *Uncle Tom's Cabin* because she could relate to the feeling of enslaved mothers whose children had been sold and taken away from them.

For Harriet Beecher Stowe, suffering united with empathy led to persistence. Her impact can be felt to this day. God is infinitely more powerful than we ask or imagine. He embraces the challenges we face and, if we are open and willing, works within us a spirit of unconditional love. This love is not weak or fragile, but strong and withstanding. This love is why we enter our places of learning each day, persistent in doing the work that will leave a legacy of positive change.

Today's Intention:

_____

_____

_____

_____

May the Lord Bless You and Keep You:

Today, may you feel Jesus' loving presence with you as you walk through your day.
In both joyful and painful experiences, may persistence be cultivated, rooted in the knowledge that God is working on your behalf.
May you never give up, holding onto the promise of Hope you find in your Savior.

Memorable Moment:

_____

_____

_____

_____

I AM WEAK

"But he said to me, 'My grace is sufficient for you, for my power is made perfect in weakness.' Therefore I will boast all the more gladly about my weaknesses, so that Christ's power may rest on me. That is why, for Christ's sake, I delight in weaknesses, in insults, in hardships, in persecutions, in difficulties. For when I am weak, then I am strong."
~ 2 Corinthians 12:9-10 (NIV)

In our first reflection together, I shared that Micah 6:8 has been my "teacher verse" ever since I was in college. While this remains to be true, as I have gained professional experience, 2 Corinthians 12:9-10 has become my go-to passage before or after my school day. Some days, I feel completely and utterly exhausted, weak beyond words of explanation. Then I read: "My power is made perfect in weakness," and sarcastically think, *You're welcome, God.*

I can't pretend to understand how this dichotomy works. In our society, weakness is not viewed as a positive attribute, but somehow our mysterious and all-knowing God uses us when we feel we have nothing left to give. Maybe we need to get to this point to truly rely on God and trust Him at His word because we don't have any other option. We have used all of the skills and knowledge we can. Our relationships are wearing thin or at risk of fraying. We are not even sure how to continue.

At this place, we are completely vulnerable and open to Jesus' leading. When we let go of control and turn our eyes to Christ, strength will rise. This is where God's work begins, when we are not the exclusive problem-solvers, decision-makers, and writers of fate. When we recognize we cannot do it on our own, He whispers, *I can work with this,* and provides limitless grace.

Today's Intention:

_____

_____

_____

_____

May the Lord Bless You and Keep You:

Today, may you be given grace in the midst of your weaknesses.
May you intimately feel the Peace that surpasses all understanding.
When your heart finds itself sinking under the heavy earth, may the
Holy Spirit remind you that this is where seeds are planted.
And may God work miraculous growth in unexpected ways.

Memorable Moment:

_____

_____

_____

_____

I AM BROKEN

"Waiting with hope is very difficult, but true patience is expressed when we must even wait for hope. I will have reached the point of greatest strength once I have learned to wait for hope."
~ George Matheson [33]

Waiting for hope. I think one of the lowest places we can find ourselves in is when we are simply waiting to feel hopeful again. We are wading through a dark, deep place. We may have experienced seasons when the only prayer we can muster is: *God, help me hope again.* We wonder if anyone can find us in this place. *Does God even exist in these broken moments? And if He does, why did He let me get to this point?*

I find comfort in George Matheson's words when he writes, *I will have reached the point of greatest strength once I have learned to wait for hope.* In some seasons, hope is a process - a journey. Perhaps we do not have words for prayer or praise. That's okay. In these times, we are given an Intercessor who prays on our behalf. "Likewise the Spirit helps us in our weakness. For we do not know what to pray for as we ought, but the Spirit himself intercedes for us with groanings too deep for words. And he who searches hearts knows what is the mind of the Spirit, because the Spirit intercedes for the saints according to the will of God" (Romans 8:26-27 ESV).

You are not broken, my friend. You are not abandoned by God. You may be experiencing a difficult season, but the Holy Spirit is stirring up strength in you to wait for hope. Jesus is here with you now, calm in the midst of the storm. Hold onto His hand and cling to Him because He is your *point of greatest strength.*

Today's Intention:

_____

_____

_____

_____

May the Lord Bless You and Keep You:

Today, may the Holy Spirit intervene on your behalf in a powerful way.
May you be given the strength to wait for hope once again.
In your brokenness, may you feel the loving mercy of our Heavenly Father.
And may you embrace the reality that His power is truly made perfect in your weakness.
You are claimed. You are loved.

Memorable Moment:

_____

_____

_____

_____

I AM WAITING

"Waiting is a period of learning. The longer we wait, the more we hear about Him for whom we are waiting."
~ Henri Nouwen [34]

I am waiting with excitement
For new buds to bloom and new ideas to form.
Earnestly seeking adventure and fresh perspective,
I step out even while I wait,
Confident that God knows the plans He has for me.

I am waiting with grief
To feel whole, healthy, and joyful once again.
My heart hurts in ways I can't express.
I wait with my Comforter,
Knowing He is with me in the time to laugh and in the time to cry.

I am waiting with curiosity,
Asking questions: *Who? What? When? Why? Where? How?*
Enjoying the mystery that is life itself.
I wonder and wait,
As God works on my behalf.

I am waiting with hope.
A brighter future is in store for this student, and thus, this world.
I have good reasons to wait with hope.
I am inextricably connected to the Author of hope,
And He is still writing.

Today's Intention:

_____

_____

_____

_____

May the Lord Bless You and Keep You:

Today, may you find meaning and purpose in your season of waiting.
May your heart be drawn closer to God in prayer, sharing your hopes and hurts.
May this time of stillness or questioning lead to learning and loving.
What are you waiting for?

Memorable Moment:

_____

_____

_____

_____

I AM HOPEFUL

"We wait in hope for the Lord; he is our help and our shield.
In him our hearts rejoice, for we trust in his holy name.
May your unfailing love rest upon us, O Lord, even as we put
our trust in you."
~ Psalm 33:20-22 (NIV)

My friend, how is your heart today?

What joys are you feeling?

What burdens are you carrying?

Feel free to take a moment to whisper them or write them down.
Our joys and burdens are important and very real. While I am
listening in spirit, empathizing with what I imagine your answers
may be, our Heavenly Father is listening to you now and knows
you deeply. He is intimately in tune with your joys, however
vibrant or subtle they are. And He yearns to carry your burdens
for you.

My friend, do you feel hopeful or hopeless today?

Or perhaps, a blending of both?

Our Lord hears your answer and meets you in this moment. He
loves you unconditionally. When we do not have everything
figured out and our to-do list isn't even close to being complete,
even here, *we wait in hope for the Lord.* He will take your hand
through this day. *Trust in His Holy Name.*

Today's Intention:

_____

_____

_____

_____

May the Lord Bless You and Keep You:

Today, may you come as you are and wait in hope for the Lord.
May you cling to the promise that He is your help and shield.
May your heart rejoice because His powerful, Holy Name is
trustworthy.
May God's unfailing love rest upon you as you approach the next
moment, putting your trust in Him.

Memorable Moment:

_____

_____

_____

_____

I AM FORGIVEN

"Forgiveness is truly the grace by which we enable another person to get up, and get up with dignity, to begin anew."
~ Desmond Tutu & Mpho Tutu [35]

It was just one of those days. You know, the one where there are endless fires to put out, no lunch break, and you are praying for a much-needed trip to the bathroom. In the midst of this, a student brought to class a small bottle of red Kool-Aid drops, most of it ending up on students' desks and all over the floor. Despite several requests from me to put it in his backpack, and a firm conversation in the hallway, he refused. My patience was wearing thin, and my voice became louder and stronger in my frustration. Surprised by my abnormal demeanor, he ran to the principal's office, and I rejoined my waiting class.

I knew I had messed up. I felt it. I acted out of character and broke trust with this student. While checking in with other students and continuing instruction, I connected with God in that moment, feeling ashamed of my behavior. I felt the words, *I have forgiven you. You don't need to carry this.* And almost unexplainably, I did feel forgiven. But I knew it didn't stop there. I needed to make it right.

When the student rejoined the class, still very angry, I calmly looked at him and asked if he could join me at my table. He agreed. I looked at him closely and said, "I want to apologize for how I handled that situation. I was feeling frustrated, and I acted in a way that I am not proud of. I should not have raised my voice to you. It probably felt really surprising that I reacted that way, didn't it?" "Yes," he responded. "I'm sorry," I said. "It's okay," he replied. I began to explain, "It's important to me that I don't take what belongs to you, but we can't have certain things in the classroom. May I keep your Kool-Aid and we can make sure it gets in your backpack before you go home?" "Yeah, that works," he said.

I was forgiven first by God, but then I needed to forgive myself and the student before we could move on. The student forgiving me was another big step that impacted his future interactions. The next day, this student did something unkind to another student. For the first time all year, he took responsibility and apologized to the other student. I almost couldn't believe it! The power of forgiveness is life changing.

Today's Intention:

_____

_____

_____

_____

May the Lord Bless You and Keep You:

Today, may you move forward in the confidence that you are forgiven.
Nothing you have ever done or could ever do will change this promise.
May the Holy Spirit fill you with freedom as you rest in this reality.
Out of this God-given grace, may you extend forgiveness to others.
And may this action become a chain reaction of love and grace.

Memorable Moment:

_____

_____

_____

_____

I AM A CHANGEMAKER

**"When you pick up a child, you change their perspective. All of a sudden, they can see the world the way you see it."
~ Walter Bond [36]**

One morning on my drive to work, I was listening to a motivational speech by Walter Bond. (I encourage you to listen to his full speech which is identified in the Notes section of this book.) While the target audience for this speech is athletes or business professionals, when I heard the words quoted above, tears filled my eyes. *That's my purpose,* I thought. *It's that simple.* Invite opportunities for students to see themselves the way Christ does: unconditionally loved and possessing limitless possibility! Where might we find these opportunities?

An eighth-grader is sitting in their Language Arts class and hates it because they do not think of themself as a reader; a previous teacher told them they would never be able to read big books.

Here's your chance. Pick them up. Change their perspective.

You ask an eleventh-grader, "What do you want to do after you graduate?" They give a sarcastic laugh, "I don't know. I can't do anything." Yesterday, someone in their family told them they would never be smart enough to make it into college.

Here's your chance. Pick them up. Change their perspective.

When you "pick up" a child, teenager, or adult, you can unexpectedly shift their perspective of the present and future. But you first need to take the action of lifting them. Every day, the Holy Spirit is orchestrating opportunities for us to notice students who are hurting and hopeless. We may not know their experiences - the limiting ideas they have accepted about themselves or what others have told them. However, we do know the truths we can tell them: messages of hope, belief, and determination, giving them an open door to see themselves with value and purpose. During the hours they are with us, we are empowered to be changemakers.

Today's Intention:

_____

_____

_____

_____

May the Lord Bless You and Keep You:

Today, may your eyes be open to those who need to be picked up.
You have the power to change someone's perspective for eternity.
May you inspire others to see them the way you do and the way Christ does.
May you be the reason someone believes they are worthy of love, belonging,
and hope.

Memorable Moment:

_____

_____

_____

_____

I AM A PROTECTOR

"Defend the weak and fatherless; uphold the cause of the poor and the oppressed. Rescue the weak and the needy; deliver them from the hand of the wicked."
~ Psalm 82:3-4 (NIV)

In most school districts toward the end of the year, there are transition meetings. The teachers of students in their current grade meet with the next grade's staff to discuss important information and class composition. One year, while in a transition meeting, we were sitting around the table and the dean asked me about my students that year. I began going down my class list, pointing out students who had incredible work ethics or particular struggles and strategies to note.

As I made my way down the list, I named a student, and before I had the chance to give my feedback, the dean interrupted saying, "Oh yes, we know about him. We flagged him already." I stopped for a moment and the Mama Bear in me came alive. This student had faced unimaginable challenges, and yet he continued to be kind, strong, and creative. Dumbfounded, I asked, "Flagged for what?" The dean alluded to physical altercations, defiant behavior, and low grades. I wondered where these assumptions originated because they were definitely not on my comment list! "I can only share my experiences with this child, but my feedback is this," I began. "He is the most resilient student I have ever taught. He grew three reading levels this year. If you are looking for an incredibly empathetic student, he is your guy. If I could pick anyone on my list who needs someone in their corner, it's this student. Whatever you do, have his back," I concluded. "Thank you. I'll make sure to share this feedback," the dean responded.

Protection can come in many forms. A vital part of our job is to protect the reputation and future of our students. Every single child deserves new opportunities and hopeful perspectives. It may mean disagreeing with assumptions and preconceived ideas. We may not be the favorite in these conversations, but remember an important reason why we have been called to this work: to advocate for our students.

Today's Intention:

_____

_____

_____

_____

May the Lord Bless You and Keep You:

May you have the courage to step in when advocacy is needed.
May you disrupt misconceptions and false judgements with truth.
On the most difficult days, may the Holy Spirit bless you with patience and hope.
In all circumstances, may you hold confidence that God is fighting on your behalf as well.

Memorable Moment:

_____

_____

_____

_____

I AM POWERFUL

"May His love pour in and through you like a river of living water. You're connected to the supernatural Source of power - the Most High God."
~ Susie Larson [37]

There are days we may feel trapped, powerless in the midst of overwhelming situations. We witness the struggles of our students and desperately want to fix it all, but so much is out of our control. We see gaping flaws in our education system, failing to support our most vulnerable students; and yet, how can we change funding, regulations, and procedures within our district or state? Perhaps, we go home at night and wonder if we are able to create any impact at all.

I will not try to sugarcoat the situation because I am there with you. We are in a profession unlike almost any other, and it is difficult. However, I do not believe God has called us to be in these positions because He intended a feeling of powerlessness or apathy. Instead, I believe He has placed us in these roles because He knows the power we *do possess* in Him.

Through the Holy Spirit, a supernatural Source of power dwells within us. We stand on this truth! The reality is if we let go of our agendas and follow God in full obedience, anything can happen. It is risky! He may place us in positions of leadership or influence. He may expect that we stand out from the crowd, and it may feel uncomfortable. But I wonder if any significant, positive change ever happened while feeling comfortable. We are much more powerful than we know because of our identity in Christ. Are you willing to risk comfort and consistency for opening your heart to the possibilities that God's plan holds?

Today's Intention:

_____

_____

_____

_____

May the Lord Bless You and Keep You:
Today, may your heart and spirit be revived!
You are traveling a difficult journey.
May you be reminded that you do not travel alone.
May the Holy Spirit empower your soul and mind to follow God
without hesitation.
May you have the courage to risk discomfort in order to live out
God's design for your life.
And may you know: you are powerful.

Memorable Moment:

_____

_____

_____

_____

I AM DISCIPLINED

"Don't you realize that in a race everyone runs, but only one person gets the prize? So run to win! All athletes are disciplined in their training. They do it to win a prize that will fade away, but we do it for an eternal prize. So I run with purpose in every step. I am not just shadowboxing. I discipline my body like an athlete, training it to do what it should. Otherwise, I fear that after preaching to others I myself might be disqualified."
~ 1 Corinthians 9:24-27 (NLT)

As one year ends and another begins, it is a common practice to set New Year resolutions. Many view a new calendar year as an invitation to set goals, create plans, and dream big! There is often a determined and disciplined spirit associated with these resolutions - a rush of motivation to develop new skills and progress forward. It's exciting! But what happens when mistakes and missed deadlines enter the scene, when life becomes busier than anticipated, and when not every plan comes to fruition?

Our reality is messy and complex. Whether we are entering a new year or not, everyday we are reminded that God welcomes us to grow in discipline, surrounded by His grace. Discipline means to train someone in obedience. Out of the same root word comes, "disciple," which means a learner or follower. When we look closely at these words, we realize discipline is all about being open to learning and obeying. When Paul describes *running with purpose in every step,* he is pointing to our purpose in Christ. We arise each morning, blessed with new grace and invited into discovery and development, following God's calling for our lives in trusting obedience.

We do it for an eternal prize. In our role as educators, what is the prize we are running toward? Perhaps, we will all answer this question in our own way today; however, I imagine a common theme is God's kingdom work. We are called and conditioned to be a light in our communities, sharing love and compassion with those around us. In opening ourselves to learning and following, we develop discipline which glorifies God.

Today's Intention:

_____

_____

_____

_____

May the Lord Bless You and Keep You:
May God cover you with His grace today.
May you be reminded of how God embraces you, your students, and all those around you.
God has given you more power over your circumstances than you realize.
May the Holy Spirit uplift you in strength and love.
And may the peace of Christ dwell in you as you take steps forward in trusting obedience.

Memorable Moment:

_____

_____

_____

_____

I AM A CONQUEROR

"If God is for us, who can be against us? ...No, in all these things we are more than conquerors through Him who loved us."
~ Romans 8:31, 37 (NIV)

What are we striving to conquer in life right now? Systems of injustice and hate? Fears of inadequacy or taking risks? Painful circumstances that feel out of our control? We may be in the midst of external struggles, monopolizing our lives and relationships. Or our fight may be internal and hidden from the world as we put on a brave face and do the next thing. Our battles are personal.

Someone once told me, "God doesn't let you lose the battle, but He does let you fight." When I heard these words, it profoundly impacted my next steps. I realized I needed to develop skills to fight the battles I was experiencing so my mind could be stronger. I prayed for growth. I worked on patience toward myself and sought out people who would encourage and walk alongside me in the areas I was (and still am) developing. At the end of the day, I reminded myself that it is okay to just be still and know that God is in control.

Another way to describe, "conquer," is to overcome. We are more than conquerors through Christ who loves us more deeply than we can comprehend. That means, not only do we overcome our challenges, we are also invited into freedom and abundance. We ultimately remain grounded in the question: *If God is for us, who can be against us?* Jesus is fighting on our behalf, and He reigns victorious! He inspires us to live victoriously and make choices that will lead to abundant life.

Today's Intention:

_____

_____

_____

_____

May the Lord Bless You and Keep You:

Today, may you be reminded of what you have conquered so far in your life, through God's power.
May you dwell on your victories and trust in Almighty God!
You are invited to humbly reflect on the areas in your life that you need to develop.
In God's grace, may you be excited and determined to make healthy choices in mind, body, and spirit.
And may your hard work ready you for battle, confident that God will never fail you.

Memorable Moment:

_____

_____

_____

_____

I AM GRITTY

"Don't burn out; keep yourselves fueled and aflame. Be alert servants of the Master cheerfully expectant. Don't quit in hard times; pray all the harder."
~ Romans 12:11-12 (MSG)

Those who have experienced struggle and press forward in the name of Jesus Christ, have some pretty gritty faith! If you ask my opinion, gritty faith is required of those who are in the field of building up and supporting our next generation. *Real Talk Time:* There is not a lot of room for lukewarm Christianity in our calling.

It often feels like we are constantly surrounded by chaos, division, and hurt. However, in the midst of the toughest times, we have the opportunity to shine the brightest because of our faith in Jesus, which reminds us: "I can do all this through him who gives me strength" (Phil. 4:13 NIV). And "My God will meet all your needs according to the riches of his glory in Christ Jesus" (Phil. 4:19 NIV). So here is my gritty reminder for you today:

God is strengthening you! When everyone is fretting and frazzled, arguing about politics and petty procedures, you will show up. You are spending these days growing stronger, finding solutions, and investing time and energy into your students. Evil forces cannot break you. Deeply harness your quiet confidence. Take the stress you feel and use it to fuel productivity. Develop plans and solutions without being asked or reminded. Keep pushing, even though you deserve a break. You can move forward and make progress without gratitude or recognition, without permission, and without regret. In doing these things, you will ignite a more significant impact than you will ever know, giving all glory to God.

Today's Intention:

_____

_____

_____

_____

May the Lord Bless You and Keep You:
Today, may you be invigorated by fresh, gritty faith.
May you put your head down, stay focused on your purpose, and do the next thing.
May the Holy Spirit caution your heart against anything that would not be an honorable use of energy.
May you lift your head up to see how God's power has been made perfect in your moments of weakness.
And may your gritty faithfulness produce outcomes beyond your wildest dreams.

Memorable Moment:

_____

_____

_____

_____

I AM AUDACIOUS

"Even if my eyes are heavy, I will push forward with audacity, and I will rise with strength at dawn."
~ Morgan Harper Nichols [38]

Even if my eyes are heavy...

Are you weary, my friend? On our journey, we have invested our time, energy, and resources. We have had sleepless nights. Our eyes have felt the tired and swollen sting from the tears we have shed. Our hearts have felt heavy and tight from the stories we've heard and the burdens we've carried.

...I will push forward with audacity...

Being audacious means the willingness to take surprising, bold, intrepidly daring risks! Perhaps it feels uncertain and uncomfortable to step forward with audacity when our eyes are heavy. When we are doing the best we can with what we have in the moment, pushing forward to take courageous risks may not even feel possible.

...I will rise with strength at dawn.

God has promised us new mercies every morning. He will provide the strength we need for the next step forward. When we dwell in His new mercies and turn to our audacious Savior for hope, we are reminded Christ rose with strength at dawn! His surprising, bold resurrection inspires our spirits with the reality that, even beyond death, God brings about life. He hears the desires of our hearts and fuels our passions for His glory. We will rise once again; perhaps still with heavy eyes, knowing we are equipped for what the day will hold. Then, we take a breath and entrust the rest to God.

Today's Intention:

_____

_____

_____

_____

May the Lord Bless You and Keep You:
Today, may you have the courage to be audacious.
When failure and heartbreak seep into your soul, may you turn your
gaze to your loving Father and embrace forgiveness and restoration.
As He holds your hand, may you rise back up to your feet and take
the next step with audacity.

Memorable Moment:

_____

_____

_____

_____

I AM RESILIENT

"We've been surrounded and battered by troubles, but we're not demoralized; We're not sure what to do, but we know that God knows what to do; We've been spiritually terrorized, but God hasn't left our side; "We've been thrown down, but we haven't been broken."
~ 2 Corinthians 4:8-9 (MSG)

One definition of resilience is the ability to recoil or spring back into shape, after bending, stretching, or being compressed. Are there areas in life right now where you feel bent? Stretched? Compressed? Perhaps it's to the point where the idea of "springing back" sounds impossible.

The Apostle Paul absolutely understood these feelings. He described being surrounded, battered, unsure, spiritually terrorized, and thrown down. *But* he was empowered to name his feelings, emotions, and very real struggles and attach a Higher Power to them. In the pain, he was still confident that God would not leave him there alone. He made bold statements, maybe even before he felt them in his heart. Following Paul's example, let's make some resilient statements for today:

We are weary from meetings, correspondence, and planning,

but we have not lost our creativity.

We have been disrespected and disheartened,

but our identity remains in Christ.

Our physical bodies may reveal our exhaustion,

but we wear the armor of God in all we do.

We may not know where our journey will lead,

but we are confident in Who guides us every step of the way.

Today's Intention:

_____

_____

_____

_____

May the Lord Bless You and Keep You:

Today, may God surprise you with His resilience in you.
May you boldly take hold of His promises over your life.
May you make courageous statements about your calling and purpose.
In the toughest moments, may you be confident that you are able to rise.
God is using your story in miraculous ways.
Just take the next step in trust.

Memorable Moment:

_____

_____

_____

_____

I AM RESCUED

"You're blessed when you feel you've lost what is most dear to you. Only then can you be embraced by the One most dear to you."
~ Matthew 5:4 (MSG)

These words in Matthew 5 are spoken by Jesus. What love our Heavenly Father has for us that He sent His Son to live on the earth, understanding and empathizing with our experiences. Jesus' purpose was to defeat the power of sin and death, and in the process, His human experience introduces us to a personal, relational Teacher.

As a baby, Christ entered into our broken world, His family in an incredibly vulnerable position. Far from their support system, Mary and Joseph became refugees soon after Jesus was born, risking everything to protect their child. Although we do not know much about many years of Jesus' life, we do know He was fully human, and therefore experienced all of the feelings we do: joy, excitement, curiosity, anger, grief, confusion, exhaustion, and loss.

God sent Jesus to offer us a relational rescue. When we are sinking, Christ bends down, takes our hand, and lifts us up. We are rescued, not by a stranger, but by a friend - One who knows what we are going through. Jesus said we are blessed when we lose what is dear to us because He knew what that felt like. He also felt the embrace of His Father and could testify to the rescuing power of God.

Today's Intention:

_____

_____

_____

_____

May the Lord Bless You and Keep You:

Wherever you find yourself in this journey, know that you are not alone.
You are understood and valued for who you are.
When you feel past the point of rescue, may you remember that Jesus went beyond death to save you.
There is no depth too deep - nor distance too far - that He has not already traveled for you.
Today, may you embrace His love and feel a breath of fresh air once more.

Memorable Moment:

_____

_____

_____

_____

I AM STILL

"He says, 'Be still, and know that I am God; I will be exalted among the nations, I will be exalted in the earth.'"
~ Psalm 46:10 (NIV)

Stillness,
Contradictory to the classroom chaos.
In the midst of movement,
Pause. Breathe. Be still.

Pause long enough to hear God's gentle voice.
Breathe long enough to inhale His Spirit.
Be still long enough to revisit your soul,
As emotions and attention shift from this way to that.

Be still and embrace courageous faith,
Discovering Christ's Kingdom in this space.
And know God's design of love for His people;
The big picture.

In our moments of pause, breathing deep and wide,
Perhaps we will speak a little less and listen a little more,
To those around us and to the Holy Spirit,
Guiding us every step of the way.

Stillness is not stagnation, but blessed assurance.

Today's Intention:

_____

_____

_____

_____

May the Lord Bless You and Keep You:
In this moment, may the Holy Spirit bless you with stillness and an understanding of God.
In the midst of many responsibilities, may you be filled with peace.
May you embrace the invitation to be still today as your gaze returns to Jesus.
In this space, may your perspective be enlightened and aligned with God's vision.

Memorable Moment:

_____

_____

_____

_____

I AM RENEWED

"But those who hope in the Lord will renew their strength. They will soar on wings like eagles; they will run and not grow weary, they will walk and not be faint."
~ Isaiah 40:31 (NIV)

How are you coming to this reflection, my friend?
What have the past days and weeks felt like?
Have you experienced unexpected blessings?
Have there been heartbreaking moments?

Allow me to ask a possibly personal question: how have you been sleeping recently? Are you well-rested or has sleep become a second thought? I ask this because I don't think we talk about sleep enough within the education profession. In my career, I have experienced many nights when I didn't want to go to sleep because my dreams would mirror - or amplify - what happened during the school day. Sleep didn't feel like rest anymore; it felt exhausting. Perhaps, this feels relatable.

Those who wait for [or rest in] the Lord will gain new strength...

God welcomes us to rest in our walking, running, weakness, and even sleeplessness. When we rest in Jesus' loving arms and interrupt our reliance on the limited amount of human energy we have, we find renewed strength, soaring on wings like eagles. Once again, we are invited to draw near to the cross and embrace the promises God has spoken over us. When it feels comfortable, take a few deep breaths and meditate on these words of renewal for your life:

I will be renewed with strength.
I will mount up with wings like eagles.
I will run and not get tired.
I will walk forward and not become weary.

Today's Intention:

_____

_____

_____

_____

May the Lord Bless You and Keep You:

Today, may the Holy Spirit bring renewed strength for your mind, body, and spirit.

May God speak His promises to you in a way you can hold deeply within your heart.

May you be given the strength to love those around you and accomplish what needs to be done.

And may the Holy Spirit stir in you an understanding of the surpassing love of Jesus.

Memorable Moment:

_____

_____

_____

_____

I AM A WARRIOR

"I have set the Lord always before me. Because he is at my right hand, I will not be shaken."
~ Psalm 16:8 (NIV)

Someone once told me, "A warrior is someone who perseveres no matter the odds or outcome." Let's allow that to sink in for a moment. Our learning spaces may not be in a literal warzone; however, we fight every day for the future of the students we serve. We may be the only ones who will stand up and advocate for these children and young adults. With weapons of truth, we fight against judgment, dehumanizing policies, and hopelessness. We are champions for our students and colleagues.

We do not fight alone. *We set the Lord always before us. He is at our right hand, and we will not be shaken.* He has built an army of advocates: teachers, paraprofessionals, bus drivers, chefs, members of administration, custodians, and supporting teams who are dedicated to making a difference for our future. When we look around us for the other warriors, we will find them.

Like a soldier trusts the soldier next to them to have their back, we are also building a foundation of belief and encouragement in one another. When someone has fallen, reach out and help them up. When someone is weary, be present with them with an empathetic spirit, creating an atmosphere of unwavering support. With this united perseverance, the possibilities for impact and progress are limitless.

Today's Intention:

_____

_____

_____

_____

May the Lord Bless You and Keep You:
Today, God has made a way before you.
In moments of joy, passion, and curiosity, may you be rooted in
God's calling for your life.
On days when you feel exhausted, sad, or uncertain, may you
remember that God has equipped you.
May you be given deep confidence that your Mighty Warrior is
before, behind, and with you.
May you be empowered to persevere in fighting for a stronger future.
And in victory, may God's glory be proclaimed in your midst!

Memorable Moment:

_____

_____

_____

_____

I AM EMPOWERED

"For I can do anything through Christ, who gives me strength."
~ Philippians 4:13 (NLT)

Today is the day for us to stand confident in God's calling for our lives! We know we are facing difficult days. The reality is: life is tough. Some days, we just need to take the next step and make it through the day. But today, I propose we stand on God's promises and walk forward in power and strength!

Our reflection verse is undoubtedly one of the most well-known Bible verses, and for good reason. The word, "anything," provides us with limitless possibilities in our lives. It is a promise from God to humanity reminding us that there are no limits to what can be accomplished through Christ who gives us the strength to do it. Whether we feel this reality or not does not change its truth. Thanks be to God!

As educators, we share this truth with our students. Even though most of us may not explicitly reference Where our strength is centered, when others witness our empowerment, perhaps they will be inspired to explore their limitless potential as well. Through prayer, we hold the hope that they are also finding their Center. Witnessing people who are empowered is contagious. It sparks the question: *Why are they excited and motivated, even on the most difficult days?* We know the answer. Today, we have an opportunity to model Christ's glory and strength in us as we live out our calling once again.

Today's Intention:

_____

_____

_____

_____

May the Lord Bless You and Keep You:
Today, may you feel empowered by the Holy Spirit.
_May you walk forward in confidence, reminded of who you represent
in your learning space._
May you be equipped to tackle any situation with love and grace.
_May you hold tightly to God's promise that you can accomplish
anything through Christ's strength._
_And may your students feel empowered by your example, leaving a
legacy of inspiration._

Memorable Moment:

_____

_____

_____

_____

I AM VICTORIOUS

"The Lord is my strength and my song; he has given me victory. This is my God, and I will praise him - my father's God, and I will exalt him."
~ Exodus 15:2 (NLT)

Today's reflection verse is a small portion of the song Moses and Miriam sang after the Israelites safely crossed the Red Sea, leaving the slavery they were captive to in Egypt. As we read the lyrics they sang in praise, consider the fears, exhaustion, and trauma the Israelites had endured in their lives. They had experienced so much suffering on their journey, and the future was still unknown to them.

In the midst of these difficulties, we hear words of confident praise and thanksgiving. *The Lord is my strength and my song; he has given me victory.* The Israelites rose out of unimaginable circumstances into victory because God was leading them to this place, and they listened and obeyed His direction. In every question, God was developing faith. In every traumatic event, God was demonstrating His own strength and resilience within the Israelites.

The promise of God's victory breathes hope into us. Victory is unfolding in our classrooms, offices, cafeterias, and playgrounds. Both visible and invisible breakthroughs are happening! When it feels as if we are captive in our circumstances, our Savior advocates on our behalf, leading us into freedom. As we follow Him, we are victorious, singing and dancing our praises!

Today's Intention:

_____

_____

_____

_____

May the Lord Bless You and Keep You:

May you claim victory in your life today.
May the Holy Spirit bless you with confident trust, knowing you will not fail.
Even when hurt, pain, and exhaustion seem to gain power, may you know
with certainty that God has gone before you to win this fight.
God is fighting on your behalf today. Live victoriously!

Memorable Moment:

_____

_____

_____

_____

Part 4
I Am
Compassionate

I AM COMPASSIONATE

"If your compassion does not include yourself, it is incomplete."
~ Jack Kornfield [39]

Out of courage, compassion is developed. Many emotion-researchers describe compassion as a feeling that surfaces when one is aware of another's suffering and is compelled to relieve that suffering. The literal meaning is, "to suffer together." As teachers, we often take on the responsibility of being problem-solvers. We strive to be generous, understanding, and encouraging. These characteristics are powerful, and perhaps even necessary to fulfill our calling. However, we may reach an unhealthy breaking point if we neglect to show ourselves the same grace and compassion we extend to others.

Some of the most outwardly compassionate people I know are also the ones who struggle with perfectionism the most. They are gracious toward everyone; and yet, when they experience failure or setbacks, it feels like the world is crumbling around them. I believe Christ invites us to embrace a grace-filled mindset. This is a season to explore God's design for compassion when it is applied internally.

God loves us unconditionally, and He is compassionate beyond our comprehension. Learning from our Heavenly Father, we give ourselves permission to sit with our discouragement and shame, naming and acknowledging their impact. Out of the grace we have been given, our hearts become more open to the joy and blessings God has prepared for us. Then, filled with the Holy Spirit, we claim the truths spoken over us: Nothing can separate us from God's love (Romans 8:39). The Lord heals the brokenhearted (Psalm 147:3). By grace we have been saved – a gift from God, not of our own works (Ephesians 2:8). Living in these promises, we move forward, extending compassion outward.

Today's Intention:

_____

_____

_____

_____

May the Lord Bless You and Keep You:
Today, may you be reminded that Christ loves you unconditionally, exactly as you are.
May the Holy Spirit comfort you in times of suffering and struggle.
As you embrace others with compassion, may you also feel surrounded by grace.
And may you find new freedom in this space of belonging and love.

Memorable Moment:

_____

_____

_____

_____

I AM GRACIOUS

"Because of the Lord's great love we are not consumed, for his compassions never fail. They are new every morning; great is your faithfulness."
~ Lamentations 3:22-23 (NIV)

In the spring of 2020, the COVID-19 pandemic transformed the world in unimaginable ways. Perspectives shifted to what was truly important in life. As the world experienced turmoil and trauma, teachers, like many others, navigated how to pick up the pieces. We learned how to teach in a completely new way. We uplifted families and students, knowing school is often the most critical support system for our young people. We searched for ways to balance our own health, protect our family's well-being, and support our communities.

During the pandemic, my theme word for my students and families was: grace. I built this into my central focus, giving permission to live graciously toward myself and others. Everyone so desperately needed an invitation to be human, taking it one day at a time in the midst of messy and complex circumstances. Perhaps this event in our history was an equalizer: an experience that affected everyone (albeit in different ways), and brought to light the importance of viewing others with a gracious spirit.

We are reminded *because of the Lord's great love, we are not consumed.* We have been shown grace by Jesus first, therefore, we have the ability to develop and demonstrate graciousness. His example shows us a path for a life of unconditional love. We all deal with struggle in our own way. There are untold stories or buried feelings, influencing how we journey through our days. Students are walking into our learning spaces with unspoken and unbelievable experiences - both positive and negative - shaping who they are. Perhaps, it's best to begin with grace. Just as Jesus extends new compassion every single morning without fail, we can also start each day anew with fresh grace toward others.

Today's Intention:

_____

_____

_____

_____

May the Lord Bless You and Keep You:

May the Lord's love intervene in powerful ways on your behalf; you will not be consumed.

By His compassions, may you be inspired to be gracious.

May the Holy Spirit provide you with grace to freely give yourself and all those around you.

And may a perspective of grace bring freedom into your heart today.

Memorable Moment:

_____

_____

_____

_____

I AM PATIENT

**"I will overlook the inconveniences of the world.
Instead of cursing the one who takes my place, I'll invite him
to do so. Rather than complain that the wait is too long, I will
thank God for a moment to pray. Instead of clinching my fist
at new assignments, I will face them with joy and courage."
~ Max Lucado [40]**

Today, if you choose, I invite you to write down these answers
for your own reflection.

Who is the most patient person you have ever met?

How do you feel when you're around that individual?

What does this person do or not do that has developed patience

within them?

Patience means to be steadfast despite conflict, chaos, or
challenges. Given the circumstances we encounter during our
days, educators certainly possess an extraordinary amount of
patience! We answer the same questions many times, mediate
student disagreements, and balance the seemingly endless
barrage of emails, meetings, and other responsibilities. At times,
we may wonder what will be the final straw - the breaking point
of our patient demeanor.

Once again, we are reminded we do not need to rely on our own
strength, gentleness, or determination. The Holy Spirit
intercedes on our behalf to provide grace for ourselves and
others when we feel we have none. As we intentionally choose
gratitude and develop an awareness of God's closeness in our
daily experiences, we will find we are less dependent on our own
patience, and more filled with the grace God has shown us all
along our journey.

Today's Intention:

_____

_____

_____

_____

May the Lord Bless You and Keep You:

When this day brings unexpected interruptions, may the Holy Spirit fill you with grace to demonstrate patience.
May you be reminded of Christ's patience toward you on difficult days.
In the midst of chaos and questions, may you show kindness in your words and actions.
May your patience be contagious, impacting the atmosphere all around you.

Memorable Moment:

_____

_____

_____

_____

I AM CALM

"This is what the Sovereign Lord, the Holy One of Israel says, 'Only in returning to me and resting in me will you be saved. In quietness and confidence is your strength.'"
~ Isaiah 30:15 (NLT)

How do you want to show up in the classroom? When you paint the ideal picture for yourself as a teacher, what does that look like? Who are teachers you have admired in your experience? What characteristics did they demonstrate that helped you feel safe in that space and excited about learning?

The learning spaces I feel most comfortable in are often the ones which have a calm, yet joy-filled atmosphere. I think anytime children or young adults are present, there has to be room for laughter and fun. Many adults and children find comfort and security in a calm, consistent space as well. When we are the facilitators of that environment, we are responsible for carrying ourselves with a sense of peace and confidence.

We are also human, which means at times we feel overwhelmed, frazzled, and out of control. This passage from Isaiah gives us a path to begin our journey to find a sense of calmness. *Only in returning to me and resting in me will you be saved. In quietness and confidence is your strength.* So today, we are invited to focus on returning and resting. When the day becomes overwhelming, we will pause, breathe, turn our gaze to the Holy One of Israel, and allow ourselves to rest our minds for a moment.

Today's Intention:

_____

_____

_____

_____

May the Lord Bless You and Keep You:
Today, may you feel an overwhelming sense of calm.
May the Holy Spirit guard your heart, mind, and learning space
against anything that will introduce toxicity.
May those around you feel comfortable and secure in your presence.
May you begin to see a ripple effect of calmness around you.
And may your inner quietness and confidence bring forth strength.

Memorable Moment:

_____

_____

_____

_____

I AM CLEAR

**"May I live this day compassionate of heart,
Clear in word, gracious in awareness,
Courageous in thought, generous in love."
~ John O'Donohue** [41]

Before we dive into our theme, I want to draw our attention to the reflection quote. John O'Donohue packed some powerful words into this one sentence! May we live our days *compassionate, clear, gracious, courageous,* and *generous.* We have already explored many of these words, reflecting on how they relate to teaching. Today, let's focus specifically on being *clear in word.*

As an attribute for teachers, clarity carries a subtlety with it. This may not be the first word that comes to mind when describing those in our profession. However, when we consider our responsibilities, we realize how often choosing transparency is the kindest method of communication. As Brené Brown often writes, "Clear is kind." [42]

Because of Christ's direction in our lives, we can be clear in our word without knowing all the answers. We can be consistent in our character and values without having made every single decision in front of us. We can be trustworthy and professional while searching. Life can be a mystery at times, and perhaps, we weren't designed to have all the answers. Trusting God's timing and provision for our awaiting adventures, we do the next right thing in kindness.

Today's Intention:

_____

_____

_____

_____

May the Lord Bless You and Keep You:
Today, may you take life one step at a time.
May you embrace transparency, showing up exactly how God
designed you to be.
May the Holy Spirit bring ideas, words, and actions of clarity.
And may your clear, consistent choices build trust with those
around you.

Memorable Moment:

_____

_____

_____

_____

I AM KIND

**"Love is for today; programs are for the future,
We are for today; When tomorrow will come we shall see
what we can do. Somebody is thirsty for water today, hungry
for food today. Tomorrow we will not have them if we don't
feed them today. So be concerned with what you can do
today."
~ Mother Teresa [43]**

What legacy do you hope to leave as an educator? When students think back to their time with you, what do you hope will be the lasting impact? If you are an administrator or in leadership, what atmosphere are you creating in your building or district? We can never know for sure what experiences will remain in our students' hearts and minds, but we can be intentional about our words and actions.

I believe one of the most powerful impressions we can leave with those around us is kindness. It may sound cliché or simple, but consider our own teachers, mentors, friends, or family. There is something special about people who leave a legacy of kindness that makes the world a much richer place. Even though the word, "kind," is used often, it is rare to find kindness shown in authentic, selfless, and joyful ways.

It is possible you may be the only teacher who leaves a positive impact for a student. I have met people who can only recall one teacher - out of over a dozen - who made them feel seen and loved. While it is heartbreaking to acknowledge, it is reality. You have an opportunity to be that teacher today and for the rest of your professional career. *Be that one.* Because, if collectively we all work toward *being that one,* then authentic kindness won't be rare anymore; it will be a daily experience.

Today's Intention:

_____

_____

_____

_____

May the Lord Bless You and Keep You:

Today, may kindness pour out of your heart like a roaring waterfall after rain.

May you be inspired by the love of Christ and the empathetic actions of others.

Regardless of your mood or the habits of others, may you choose kindness today.

And may God use your faithfulness to change many lives for eternity.

Memorable Moment:

_____

_____

_____

_____

I AM A NURTURER

"God wants us to grow up, to know the whole truth and tell it in love - like Christ in everything. We take our lead from Christ, who is the source of everything we do. He keeps us in step with each other. His very breath and blood flow through us, nourishing us so that we will grow up healthy in God, robust in love."
~ Ephesians 4:15-16 (MSG)

When you hear the word, "nurture," what words or images come to mind?

When I reflect on this word, a specific painting comes to mind. It's one my mom used to show me when I was little. The image is of Jesus and four children around him. All of the children are looking up to Jesus. Jesus is earnestly and devotedly looking into the face of one of the children, her face gently held in His hands.

More times than I can remember, I watched my mom use this framed picture in a special way. If there was a group of young people together for a church activity, my mom would bring this picture around to each child and ask, "Who is this?" pointing to Jesus. The child would respond, "That's Jesus!" Then she would say, "And who is this?" pointing to the child in the picture whose face is in Jesus' hands. The child would respond, "That's me." "Yes, it is," my mom would reply. "And nothing can change that."

Jesus' embrace of this young child in the picture looks like nurture to me. My mom's reminder of each child's identity and value looks like nurture to me. How does nurture look in your learning space today?

Today's Intention:

_____

_____

_____

_____

May the Lord Bless You and Keep You:

Today, may you feel nourished and nurtured in the deep love of Jesus.
May you walk in confidence, knowing He will provide for all your needs.
May you feel drawn to unconditionally love those around you.
May you nurture the children God has blessed you with, so they may feel
safe, known, and embraced in your presence.

Memorable Moment:

_____

_____

_____

_____

I AM CURIOUS

"There is no belief so strong that it cannot be set aside temporarily to learn from someone who disagrees."
~ Nedra Glover Tawwab [44]

What will the day hold before me?

What discoveries will I make?

What am I waiting to explore?

What questions will surface as I embrace curiosity?

Am I open to searching?

Who is this future in front of me, sitting in my classroom?

What are their hopes and dreams?

Why is she so angry?

Why is he so sad?

How can I connect and learn more?

What is God nudging me to change about my habits and

mindsets?

Are my heart and mind open to new possibilities?

Am I stuck in patterns because they are comfortable?

Maybe today, I will not try to answer the wonderings.

Maybe today, I will just be curious.

Today's Intention:

_____

_____

_____

_____

May the Lord Bless You and Keep You:

Today, may your mind become an open vessel for exploration.
May you invite new questions and allow ideas to simmer.
May you look around your space with curiosity.
May you have the courage to confront perspectives and habits the
Holy Spirit is guiding you to question.
And may Jesus defeat any fear that hinders you from fully embracing
God's truth for His people.

Memorable Moment:

_____

_____

_____

_____

I AM UNDERSTOOD

"A teacher knows. No computer or system or standardized test can look into a child's eyes and recognize true understanding. A teacher does that."
~ Rafe Esquith [45]

What a feeling it is to be understood! When we are with someone who can relate to our experiences, dreams, and concerns, we feel vulnerable and safe at the same time. We find comfort in the truth that the greatest Teacher who has ever walked the earth understands us completely.

Jesus knows us better than we know ourselves. He looks into our eyes and sees the doubt, fatigue, frustration, and pain. He also knows the hope, passion, joy, and determination we have in us. He meets us in these moments and listens, promising to be with us as we continue on our journey, no matter where the path may lead.

Our reflection quote, written by the inspirational teacher, Rafe Esquith, illustrates our unique and invaluable role in the lives of children and young adults. Just as we are understood in Christ, we are called to seek greater awareness of our students and colleagues. The more we grow in our faith, understanding our Heavenly Father's character, the more the Holy Spirit fills us with knowledge, providing insight, leading us in wisdom, and guiding our words and actions throughout the day.

Today's Intention:

_____

_____

_____

_____

May the Lord Bless You and Keep You:

You are understood, my friend. You are not alone.
Your thoughts, feelings, passions, and worries matter deeply to God.
Today, may you feel a close connection with God and others.
And may you find curiosity to ask questions in order to understand
others better.

Memorable Moment:

_____

_____

_____

_____

I AM VULNERABLE

"We have spoken freely to you, Corinthians, and opened wide our hearts to you. We are not withholding yours from us. As a fair exchange - I speak to you as my children - open wide your hearts also."
~ 2 Corinthians 6:11-13 (NIV)

Teaching and type 1 diabetes is a bittersweet combination. On the first day of every school year, I tell my students about my disease in case they are wondering where the beeps on my insulin pump are coming from, or why I am drinking apple juice while teaching a math lesson. I always hope it doesn't make me a less impactful teacher, and many days, it has left me feeling like a teacher my students don't deserve - a teacher with defects. This is a vulnerable place to be. However, I have had many moments where I have seen the "sweet" in the midst of the bitter.

One day, while reading a book about Temple Grandin with a small group of students, one asked me, "Is it hard having diabetes?" I looked at her and said, "Honestly, yes. Some days are good and some days are hard. But on a hard day, I always know that soon I'm going to have another good day, so I just have to get through it." The student nodded, and we continued reading.

Our children need to see humanness and vulnerability modeled. They are growing up in a time where they see "perfection" displayed on every form of media around them. If they don't witness how adults handle hardship, they will grow up thinking they are alone in their feelings of struggle and imperfection. Let's risk being vulnerable with one another and with our children. It may result in an impact far beyond our knowledge.

Today's Intention:

_____

_____

_____

_____

May the Lord Bless You and Keep You:

Today, may the Holy Spirit give you peace and freedom to be vulnerable. May you know deep in your soul you are not less worthy because you experience struggle.
May God's design for vulnerability be revealed to you; for when you are vulnerable, connections are deepened with one another and with God. May God use your example to help others feel seen, known, and loved, cultivating compassion within your space.

Memorable Moment:

_____

_____

_____

_____

I AM TIRED

"Let us not become weary in doing good, for at the proper time we will reap a harvest if we do not give up."
~ Galatians 6:9 (NIV)

The Apostle Paul makes it sound easy, doesn't he? We may feel tired, energy-drained, and at the end of our rope. We look for comfort and read: *Let us not become weary in doing good.* For many, these Holy words may provide immediate blessing and empowerment, exactly what is needed in that moment. However, sometimes Scripture may not have an immediate physical effect. Our spirits may find refreshment, but our bodies and minds remain so very tired.

I believe Paul understood this, too. Perhaps, he wrote these letters to build up his own spirit as much as his target audience. In all the trials and persecution he experienced, did Paul need someone to remind him not to become weary? Not to give up hope? As teachers, we also do this: we offer the words and gestures we so desperately crave for ourselves. Our bodies and minds may become overwhelmed, but being weary in doing good is different than being tired. We need to be intentional about rest and how we take care of ourselves so we don't give up in the long run.

Jesus' ministry was the most impactful calling in the history of the universe, reaping a harvest we continue to witness today. For understandable reasons, He was tired. *And He rested.* He napped in the midst of storms. He took time away after witnessing a need and providing food to thousands of people. He accepted support from others. We are allowed to do the same. We have permission to take time to rest. We are not selfish or defeated if we need to step away from the classroom to refresh our heart and soul. We do not need to have hit a breaking point in order to begin a healing journey. We will be present to reap the harvest if we listen to the Holy Spirit's leading and give ourselves grace to rest when we need it.

Today's Intention:

_____

_____

_____

_____

May the Lord Bless You and Keep You:

May you find freedom to give yourself permission to rest.
May you proactively seek out moments of refreshment.
May Jesus Himself clear away any guilt or shame you carry for
creating room in your life to breathe.
Your students, colleagues, community, and family are healthier when
you choose to be healthier.
May you take time to sit close to your Heavenly Father, and just be.

Memorable Moment:

_____

_____

_____

_____

I AM ANXIOUS

"Do not be anxious about anything, but in everything by prayer and pleading with thanksgiving let your requests be made known to God. And the peace of God, which surpasses all comprehension, will guard your hearts and minds in Christ Jesus."
~ Philippians 4:6-7 (NASB)

Internal tornadoes. When I have no other words, this is how I describe rising anxieties. Growing up in Minnesota, I was accustomed to tornadoes. Whether at home or in a school building, I engaged in conversations about staying proactive and safe. I understood the protocol:

Recognize the signs a tornado may be approaching.
Gather the most important items. Prioritizing is key.
Listen for the sirens.
If the alarm sounds, go to a basement or another sheltered
    location, pick a comforting activity, and pray for safety.
Wait it out. Return above ground when it is safe.

In my experience, increasing anxiety is not unlike the threat of a tornado touching down. Perhaps a similar protocol may be applicable to our internal tornadoes as well:

Recognize the signs of escalating anxiety, depression, or
    exhaustion.
Prioritize what is most important to you.
When it is getting to a critical level, listen for the alarm and get to a
    safer location. This may look like taking a day off or finding
    childcare after work to embrace some space for yourself.
Wait it out. Sometimes the storms feel like they will go on forever,
    but this particular season will pass in time.
Pray. Seek connection with God in all situations.

Today's Intention:

_____

_____

_____

_____

May the Lord Bless You and Keep You:

In the midst of rising anxieties, may you be enveloped in God's protection and peace.

May you stay in close communication with your Comforter, expressing your concerns, gratitude, and dreams for the future.

May the peace of God become evident in ways you have never imagined. And may your mind and heart be guarded by Jesus.

Memorable Moment:

_____

_____

_____

_____

I AM BALANCED

**"Pay attention to the external Source and the Internal power
will be there."
~ Oswald Chambers [46]**

External and internal,
A constant balancing act.
Outward pressure, responsibility, and timelines.
Inward desire, emotion, and curiosity.
How do we find balance between the two?

External Source
Pay attention to our divine Creator and Redeemer of all.
What purposes are being positioned at this moment?
Who is being gathered in love to collaborate on this journey?
What power and strength are freely given to use in this calling!

Internal Power
The Holy Spirit resides here,
Within our dreams, feelings, and questions.
Here, power is fueled by the One who spoke life into action.
Here, peace dwells beyond the measure of comprehension.
Here, balance breathes deeply,
Intertwined with our external Source,
Capable of far more than we ask or think.

Today's Intention:

_____

_____

_____

_____

May the Lord Bless You and Keep You:

May you notice areas where you have been holding on too tightly.
May you feel the freedom to let go and relax.
May God position people in your midst who will walk alongside you in both joyful and challenging seasons.
May you develop a balanced approach to your professional and personal life.
Today, may the Holy Spirit lead you into deeper trust as you focus on your external Source.

Memorable Moment:

_____

_____

_____

_____

I AM HEARTBROKEN

How long, Lord, must I call for help, but you do not listen? Or cry out to you, "Violence!" but you do not save? Why do you make me look at injustice? Why do you tolerate wrongdoing? Destruction and violence are before me; there is strife, and conflict abounds.
~ Habakkuk 1:2-3 (NIV)

The privilege and joy of our calling also comes with the pain of witnessing tremendous trauma and hardships: violence, injustice, wrongdoing, destruction, strife, and conflict. No community is free from this burden, no matter the zip code. It is important to acknowledge, when we make the choice to invest in and build relationships with our students, we will take remnants of our students' hardships home with us. This is real and difficult, which is why we recognize it today. We have a challenging task in front of us.

In our reflection verses, we read a very personal conversation between Habakkuk and God. Habakkuk was fed up. He was committed to his prophetic calling, but he felt exhausted. His heart was breaking over the violence, injustice, and destruction he was witnessing. I can imagine he felt alone in pursuing righteousness and service. Out of this, we hear his cries of desperation to God.

Perhaps, our reflection cannot end with answers or challenges resolved. These verses serve as a reminder that God listens to our pleas when we are heartbroken. We do not need to come before Him with perfect language and happy hearts. Our Savior embraces our questions, confusion, anger, and exhaustion. He strengthens us during the tough moments, while we rest in His mighty, listening presence.

Today's Intention:

_____

_____

_____

_____

May the Lord Bless You and Keep You:

Today, may you feel the realness of God's love for you.
May you remain centered in God's unconditional love for all people.
May the Holy Spirit guard your heart from creating barriers and taking this journey alone.
Instead, may you invite God to go before you, with you, and behind you.
You cannot fix it all, my friend. And yet, you are still enough.

Memorable Moment:

_____

_____

_____

_____

I AM SAD

"Jesus wept."
~ John 11:35 (NIV)

In this short verse, we discover so much about who our Savior is. Our story from John's Gospel is about Jesus' good friend, Lazarus, who has died, and Jesus is grieving with Mary, Martha, and their relatives. The story ends with Jesus raising Lazarus from the dead – a miraculous, breakthrough miracle! So we may wonder, why is Jesus weeping? Doesn't He know what He is about to accomplish? Surely He understands the capacity of His power. Jesus cries because, in that moment, He feels sad. He was overwhelmed by grief, and instead of running to the tomb to fix the problem, He allowed Himself to stay in that space of sadness and *just feel*. This is part of being human.

On some days, there is no other word to describe the feeling. We just feel sad. We may not even understand what prompted the feeling - why we are crying or why we cannot lift ourselves up from this low mood. We desperately want to feel joy and hope again, but it does not feel like our reality at this time.

As much as it may not sound helpful, I think it is okay to pause and be still in our moments of sadness. If we wake up in the morning and our hearts feel heavy before the day even begins, it may be helpful to name our sadness to God while listening to a meaningful song on our commute to work. At the end of a long day, we may give ourselves the grace to sit and have a quiet moment or a releasing cry. Acknowledging our humanness is an important step in showing empathy to others. We cannot show true compassion to those experiencing sadness without first embracing it ourselves.

Today's Intention:

_____

_____

_____

_____

May the Lord Bless You and Keep You:

Today, may you give yourself permission to feel.
In your joyful moments, may you feel blessed and excited to bless others!
When sadness surfaces and fills your heart, may the Holy Spirit bring grace and hold you in this time.
And may your empathy and understanding for others grow through your own experiences.

Memorable Moment:

_____

_____

_____

_____

I AM PRAYERFUL

"Pray now; Draw on the grace of God in the moment of need."
~ Oswald Chambers [47]

Prayer, our invitation to communicate directly with God, is an incredibly powerful resource to draw on as we fulfill our teaching responsibilities. There is a supernatural connection between God, ourselves, and our students. Prayer brings our awareness to God's presence and Sovereignty, and it builds compassion within us. However, like all forms of communication, prayer requires patience and practice.

During my first year of teaching, I remember intentionally praying for my students daily. If there was an activity to distribute before they arrived, I would take that opportunity to pray for each child as I placed the paper on their desk. Sometimes, I would mentally pray over our Morning Meeting sharing question or a special read-aloud book. In the midst of a particularly challenging year, praying in the moment of need strengthened every part of my school day. It began to feel like prayer breaths, as simple as: *God, give me patience. Jesus, help. Holy Spirit, walk with me.*

Over the next several years, I slowly and subconsciously shifted away from these practices. I can't identify a particular reason for this, but I know as a result, I became more self-focused and overwhelmed. This is an area I would like to continue to develop in my practice. Prayer is so real and vulnerable. Communication with our Heavenly Father is purposeful, whether abstract and messy or intentional and specific. Praise be to God that we are welcomed into a close, authentic relationship with our listening, loving God.

Today's Intention:

_____

_____

_____

_____

May the Lord Bless You and Keep You:
Today, may you feel a close connection with God.
May you feel nudges to talk with Him throughout the day.
May you come before Him in gratitude for the blessings you notice.
May you seek Jesus and rely on His strength in the difficult moments when your patience is wearing thin.
His power is made perfect in weakness. He will intercede on your behalf.

Memorable Moment:

_____

_____

_____

_____

I AM A LISTENER

"Then [Elijah] was told, 'Go stand on the mountain at attention before God. God will pass by.' A hurricane wind ripped through the mountains and shattered the rocks before God, but God wasn't to be found in the wind; after the wind an earthquake, but God wasn't in the earthquake; and after the earthquake fire, but God wasn't in the fire; and after the fire a gentle and quiet whisper."
~ 1 Kings 19:11-12 (MSG)

Are we listening?
Do we risk opening our hearts to new voices and perspectives?
Do we accept others' experiences with belief and compassion?
Are we showing up and being present when someone is ready to share?
Are we the only ones who will listen?

When you listen, what do you hear?
Do you hear unexpected struggles, new beginnings, or unimaginable resilience?
Do you notice innocent laughter, creative joy, and natural kindness?
Do you hear Christ's whisper in your daily routines?
Do you feel the Holy Spirit nudging you to lean in closer and search deeper?

Gentle whispers are all around us. God wasn't in the wind or the earthquake or the fire. He was in the whisper. He *is* in the whisper. The question is: *Are we listening?*

Today's Intention:

_____

_____

_____

_____

May the Lord Bless You and Keep You:
Today, may you practice intentional listening.
May you risk feeling uncomfortable, for compassionate listening requires
vulnerability.
In cluttered moments, may your heart be still enough to hear the whispers.
And may those around you feel heard and known when they are with you,
drawing them closer to your Listener.

Memorable Moment:

_____

_____

_____

_____

I AM TRUSTING

"Focus on enjoying Me and all that I am to you - even though your circumstances scream for resolution. Refuse to obsess about your problems and how you are going to fix them. Instead, affirm your trust in Me; wait hopefully in My Presence, and watch to see what I will do."
~ Sarah Young [48]

A few years ago in February, my friend and I visited several state parks along Lake Superior. If you have had the pleasure of visiting Minnesota, you know this is a bitterly cold time of the year to go hiking. However, it was absolutely worth it! We saw waterfalls, rivers, and caves that were frozen over. It was breathtaking to behold!

Even more amazing was when we paused to look closely at the frozen nature around us. We noticed, underneath a layer of ice, water was still flowing. There were areas where we could see rushing water breaking through or strong currents racing under sheets of ice. These were powerful, majestic bodies of water, but because of the extreme conditions around them, they could not show the full potential of their power. Just for this season.

Water continues to flow beneath the surface. Spring will come. Warm air and light will bring a new energy, break the barriers of ice, and invite new life into the rushing rivers. Nature is inextricably connected to its Creator. It trusts His faithfulness and timing without hesitation. In the midst of our current season, we too are surrounded by His grace and purpose. We trust all things will melt, grow, and bloom in due time. And even in the waiting, God still reveals beauty around us now.

Today's Intention:

_____

_____

_____

_____

May the Lord Bless You and Keep You:

Today, may you be reminded of God's faithfulness in your life.
May you recognize the challenges you are facing will fade and wash away.
In the midst of bitterly cold moments, may you pause to reflect on the
continual flow of miracles and blessings.
May your trust be strengthened as you focus on our Heavenly Creator.
And may spring be fast-approaching, bringing with it beauty, power, and life
once more.

Memorable Moment:

_____

_____

_____

_____

I AM PEACEFUL

**"The peace of God is not the comfortable avoidance of all
stress. True peace has room enough for all difficulties."
~ Richard Rohr** [49]

Peace can be described as tranquility, freedom, or harmony. We
often go to great lengths in our journey to find serenity. We may
find ourselves defining peace as *the comfortable avoidance of all
stress,* expecting we will only feel peaceful if and when we can rid
our lives of stress. Perhaps we believe peace will become a
reality when we have all of the answers, the conferences are
over, and everything is checked off of our to-do lists.

We hear messages telling us peace is found in the pristine
conditions of our house or classroom. Surpassing inner
tranquility is found in yoga classes and essential oils. (These
examples are from personal experience!) In these scenarios,
peace is entirely dependent on us and on our actions, but it was
never intended to be. While these offer helpful benefits and they
may be avenues in which God is at work, the peace of God is not
contingent on these factors.

God meets us here – in the messy, chaotic, or at times
dysfunctional parts of who we are - and promises comfort in this
very moment. Jesus, our Prince of Peace, invites us into harmony
and grace and through our current circumstances. *True peace has
room enough for all difficulties.* There is room for imperfection,
questions, and weariness. We can begin to feel peace in these
places when we bring our awareness to God, our true source of
wellness.

Today's Intention:

_____

_____

_____

_____

May the Lord Bless You and Keep You:

Today, may you be given Christ's peace which surpasses all understanding.
May you have assurance that God is in control of every situation.
May the Holy Spirit bring to mind times when you felt truly peaceful and use these memories to fill your heart with joy.
And may God enter into your day, providing messages of comfort and truth as you journey forward.

Memorable Moment:

_____

_____

_____

_____

I AM GROWING

"So then neither the one who plants nor the one who waters is anything, but God who causes the growth."
~ 1 Corinthians 3:7 (NASB)

Growth is a fascinating concept. When I think about growth, I immediately picture sprouting and blooming plants - the hue of flowers peeking from buds. However, this isn't the only stage of progress; growth is a tough and timely process. A seed is positioned in the dark first. I wonder if it can feel the weight of the dirt above its head, as I do at times. Does it know, in those dark moments, its roots are extending? Can it sense being slowly pushed toward the surface? When rain falls and the soil is drenched, I wonder if the seed believes it is drowning. Does it know the water will bring life and strength?

For this vulnerable seed, I wonder if minutes feel like weeks, days, or decades, as it waits to feel the sun. When it is underground, does it know the sun exists, or is it just using its energy and focus to extend a root a little further and reach a little higher? It must be hard work. How long will it take? Every seed grows in its own time. In the end, the seed will spread its growing roots and a stem will form, standing strong, using all of the nutrients it has been given. One day, it may grow a centimeter, another day an inch. There are patterns, but no one can predict growth perfectly.

In our own lives, we may feel like the seed, still waiting and working to break through the heaviness above us. Or perhaps we are in a season of joy, blessing, and contentment, noticing sprouts, buds, and beautiful flowers all around us. Wherever we are in this growing journey, we are reminded God is causing the growth. Our Holy Gardener is actively nourishing and working the land in our lives. Our joys, sorrows, questions, and decisions are in His trustworthy timing.

Today's Intention:

_____

_____

_____

_____

May the Lord Bless You and Keep You:
_In whatever season you find yourself today, may you have an overwhelming sense of God's timing and peace.
If you are in darkness, the dirt weighing heavy above you, may you trust that work is happening beneath the surface.
If you are stretching and growing in the light of the sun, may you use the Son's energy to create energy, nourishment, and beauty to share with others._

Memorable Moment:

_____

_____

_____

_____

I AM WORTHY

"The greatest challenge for most of us is believing that we are worthy [of love and belonging] now, right this minute. Worthiness doesn't have prerequisites."
~ Brené Brown [50]

I will be vulnerable with you and share that I have always struggled with feeling worthy. I don't think I realized it until I became an adult, but unworthiness has always lingered beneath the surface, revealing itself in ways I did not understand for a long time. I am still working on growing in this area.

How do you feel about embracing your worthiness? Do you feel worthy of others' love, belonging, devotion, and care? It can be challenging to embrace. As we have done before, today let's engage in a practice together. Even before we feel truly worthy, we can say or write statements of truth based on our identity in Christ.

I am worthy of belonging no matter how I look or the amount of independence I have.

I am worthy of love no matter what actions I take or the tasks I accomplish.

I am worthy of forgiveness because Christ has claimed me as His own and has forgiven me first.

I am worthy of freedom and fun because God has gifted me with so many blessings to enjoy.

I am worthy of creativity because God has designed sparks in my soul, making the world a brighter place.

Today's Intention:

_____

_____

_____

_____

May the Lord Bless You and Keep You:
You are worthy of the calling God has set before you.
Today, may you live as one worthy of this honorable responsibility.
May the Holy Spirit deepen your understanding of your value to God.
You are a worthy Kingdom subject, no matter your past, present, or future.
You are claimed and celebrated by the King of Kings.
May you step forward, confident in this Hope.

Memorable Moment:

_____

_____

_____

_____

I AM MINDFUL

"Finally, brothers and sisters, whatever is true, whatever is noble, whatever is right, whatever is pure, whatever is lovely, whatever is admirable—if anything is excellent or praiseworthy—think about such things. Whatever you have learned or received or heard from me, or seen in me—put it into practice. And the God of peace will be with you."
~ Philippians 4:8-9 (NIV)

"Mindset" is a common word we use in the field of education. In her research, Carol Dweck (among others) speaks to the power of having a growth mindset as opposed to a fixed mindset in learning. What I enjoy so much about educational research is how it pairs well with our lives of faith. Do we have a fixed or growth mindset when it comes to our faith?

Mindfulness transforms our mindset. When we are mindful, we are reflective of the messages we tell ourselves within the environment around us. In Philippians, we are reminded of what to focus on in order to develop a healthy mentality: *whatever is true, noble, right, pure, lovely, admirable, excellent, praiseworthy - think about these things*. This does not mean we should avoid messy or difficult topics; rather, when we ground our thinking in these qualities of integrity, we are better equipped to navigate challenging conversations or situations.

In response to problems, we provide noble solutions. In all contexts, we treat others with loveliness, attempting to listen and empathize with all. We are honest and unashamed, building others up instead of tearing them down. With a God-inspired mindset, our optimism is not fake or of our own doing. Our hope comes from our connection with Christ and the work we do in His name.

Today's Intention:

_____

_____

_____

_____

May the Lord Bless You and Keep You:
Today, may you be reflective of your mindset.
Your mindset is a gift that can be used to anchor your focus and decisions.
May you be disciplined to protect this mindset.
May you consider the world around you from God's perspective.
And may you find freedom in seeing others through a lens of loveliness.

Memorable Moment:

_____

_____

_____

_____

I AM FREE

"Now the Lord is the Spirit, and where the Spirit of the Lord is, there is freedom."
~ 2 Corinthians 3:17 (NIV)

My friend, today my prayer for you is that, through the Holy Spirit, you would feel open and free. I invite you to embrace a moment to read and pray these words over yourself.

I choose to live free.

Christ gave up His life, so I could have freedom in mine.

Freedom to love deeply and take risks,

Freedom to be creative and show compassion.

I am forgiven, so I may forgive others.

I can be free from the weight of people's expectations,

Free of the burden of the past, and

Free from the ash of my own sin.

When I no longer hold onto these burdens,

I am free to serve others,

Encourage and build up those around me,

Embrace the love of Christ in my life,

Listen with an open mind and heart,

Following Christ's example, while chasing my calling.

Today's Intention:

_____

_____

_____

_____

May the Lord Bless You and Keep You:

Today, may you feel an overwhelming sense of freedom come over you.
May you be free from the burdens that have been weighing on you for far too long.
May you reach out and grab hold of God's amazing grace for your life.
May you be inspired to walk - no, RUN forward in this freedom.
In hope and faith, may you stand firm when you feel overwhelmed by enemy forces.
Because of Jesus, you have already overcome.

Memorable Moment:

_____

_____

_____

_____

I AM REFRESHED

**"The Lord is my shepherd, I lack nothing.
He makes me lie down in green pastures, he leads me beside
quiet waters, he refreshes my soul. He guides me along the
right paths for his name's sake."
~ Psalm 23:1-3 (NIV)**

Imagine coming before God feeling uncertain and exhausted. You find a quiet space and whisper, *Jesus, I don't know what to do anymore. I feel tired and lost. Help me find myself again. Lead me closer to you.*

Through some tears and heavy breaths, you feel a Presence. A Voice speaks words of promise and hope: "Take my hand, my dear one. Let me lead you beside quiet waters today. It is here with Me that you find yourself again. Here you are reconnected to your joy and passion. In peaceful green pastures, you can rest, releasing the façade you've created to conceal from others the hurts and struggles you experience. Here you are seen and known for who you are. You are worthy of love and belonging."

"Walk along this path with Me," Jesus continues. "I am renewing your strength - mind, body, and spirit. Can you hear the rush of the water as it is naturally moving forward? Put your hand in the stream. Can you feel the pull of its current? That is Me. The water does not choose to chase the rocks or curve around the bends; it is empowered by its Creator." Jesus pauses to look into your eyes. "Refreshing and renewing your soul is just as natural to Me as guiding the water down its river-paths. You have been created for purposes beyond your understanding. Take my hand in trust today. I will not abandon you, but instead bless you with strength, joy, peace, and love for your journey ahead."

Today's Intention:

_____

_____

_____

_____

May the Lord Bless You and Keep You:
Today, may you be refreshed in the promise that you do not walk this path alone.
May you feel comforted by your Shepherd who cares deeply about your heart and soul.
Even in the midst of responsibilities, may you be given a moment to rest in Jesus' gracious arms.
May you watch and listen for God's direction.
May your soul be refreshed for the work He has called you to do.

Memorable Moment:

_____

_____

_____

_____

I AM A NOURISHER

"This is a large work I've called you into, but don't be overwhelmed by it. It's best to start small. Give a cool cup of water to someone who is thirsty, for instance. The smallest act of giving or receiving makes you a true apprentice. You won't lose out on a thing."
~ Matthew 10:42 (MSG)

Think of a time you felt extravagantly nourished. This could be physical, spiritual, or emotional nourishment. (Once again, you may find it helpful to write down your thoughts for later reflection.)

I feel nourished in two main ways. First, spending time in nature always fills my hungry soul. Whether that be while exploring the woods in Minnesota or when sitting on an ocean beach in Florida, I feel closest to God when I am in nature. Secondly, I feel nourished when I am surrounded by people who love me deeply. Add some good homemade food to that community, and my cup overfloweth!

Our school buildings are often places of nourishment for many students. When they enter these walls, they are filled with food, love, knowledge, and belonging. I am comforted by this translation of Jesus' words to His disciples: *This is a large work I've called you into, but don't be overwhelmed by it. It's best to start small. Give a cool cup of water to someone who is thirsty.* This grounds us in our purpose. We are reminded we don't have to do it all. We can start small and look around us for those who need a kind action of nourishment today.

Today's Intention:

_____

_____

_____

_____

May the Lord Bless You and Keep You:

Today, may you be blessed with nourishment, whether through a warm meal, a deep conversation with a friend, or a good night of rest. May you view your school as a space of nourishment for those who work and learn there.

The Holy Spirit is not limited by location, resources, or policies. Anchored in God's love, may your words and actions be a channel to nourish others.

Memorable Moment:

_____

_____

_____

_____

I AM INCLUSIVE

"[Jesus said] You decide according to what you can see and touch. I don't make judgements like that. But even if I did, my judgment would be true because I wouldn't make it out of the narrowness of my experience but in the largeness of the One who sent me, the Father."
~ John 8:15-16 (MSG)

I invite you to reflect on the following words in a meditative style today. It may be helpful to read this piece three or more times, allowing the Holy Spirit to guide how you may grow in inclusion.

Open arms and open heart,
However they enter.

All abilities and all passions.
Languages known and unknown.
Questions and answers.
Secure and scared.
Hungry and full.
Motivated and defeated.
Alone and surrounded.
Funny and quiet.
Seen and hidden.

On good days and bad,
With open arms and an open heart,
We include and embrace all who enter.
For in this space, they are all the same:
Children of God.

Today's Intention:

_____

_____

_____

_____

May the Lord Bless You and Keep You:

May you be blessed by all who enter your space, bringing unique gifts, strengths, and needs with them.

May the Holy Spirit generously give you wisdom, empathy, and love for those around you.

May everyone around you feel seen, known, valued, and included.

And may your invitation be the spark that ignites a community of love and belonging.

Memorable Moment:

_____

_____

_____

_____

I AM GENTLE

**"Nothing is won by force. I choose to be gentle.
If I raise my voice, may it be only in praise.
If I clench my fist, may it only be in prayer.
If I make a demand, may it be only of myself."
~ Max Lucado** [51]

What images or words do you associate with the word, "gentle"?

Most likely, many ideas are coming to mind, depending on our experiences and perspectives. I wonder if the word, "powerful," entered our thinking. I believe gentleness holds incredible power. Someone who demonstrates authentic gentleness has developed the discipline, mental stamina, and inner power it requires to treat others tenderly.

In our reflection quote for today, Max Lucado lists attributes and examples of gentleness. These are not easy to accomplish! Yet, his insights offer us an important perspective in our calling as educators. We could turn these statements around and consider: does productivity occur when I am forceful, raise my voice in anger, clench my fist, and make a demand toward others? Am I displaying Christ's light when these are my go-to characteristics?

We know as Christians and educators, we are called to be bold advocates, seeking justice, loving mercy, and walking humbly with God. The Holy Spirit moves us to be strong and grounded in many areas. Developing gentleness in our demeanor does not equate to passivity or fragility. Rather, when we grow an inner compassion and understanding for others' experiences, we make a demand of ourselves that we will not sit on the sidelines, but instead proclaim God's vision for His people. When we choose gentleness, we begin with praise toward God, prayer for our world, and renewed dedication to our calling.

Today's Intention:

_____

_____

_____

_____

May the Lord Bless You and Keep You:

May you seek gentleness today for yourself and for all those around you.
May the Holy Spirit strengthen your tender soul, empathizing with the needs
in your midst.
In unexpected moments, may you be given grace and patience, Christ's
peace filling your heart.
May you recognize the powerful integrity that aligns with gentleness.
And may your spirit-inspired words be filled with truth, praise, and honor.

Memorable Moment:

_____

_____

_____

_____

I AM AN ACTIVIST

"Injustice is not a right and left issue. It's a right and wrong issue. And politics often involve justice and injustice because politics influence policies that impact people...and people always matter to God."
~ Rev. Eugene Cho [52]

I want to begin by acknowledging our quote for today, which may have caught you off guard a bit. I am not a politics writer, but I am a *real talk* writer. We have explored many areas throughout our reflections, all themes which mirror what we experience in our educational positions. The reality is that our roles are affected by policies, whether that be local or national, formal or informal. We can get lost in the chaos and conviction of policies, unless we intentionally bring our focus back to our calling.

We are called to *do justice, love mercy, and walk humbly with God.* How I wish our policies resulted from these three actions! Some days, I have all of the words to express what I am witnessing around me. Other days, I am left with painful silence - whispers of a prayer - in quiet and vulnerable faith knowing somewhere, there is hope. As injustice in our communities and in the world weighs on our hearts, let us take a moment to refocus on God and His design for humanity once again.

Perhaps, let's begin with a prayer:

Father of all, we pray for healing. Inspire humanity to explore humility. We pray for Your children to be truly seen and heard. Teach us to live how Christ lived: eyes open to the needs around Him. Bring about change in our world and a change in our hearts, so we may begin with love. Begin with listening. Begin with acceptance. Quiet our hearts to hear Your voice. Then enliven and embolden our voices to speak Your words of love, mercy, and justice. Amen.

Today's Intention:

_____

_____

_____

_____

May the Lord Bless You and Keep You:

Today, may your faith become active in the face of injustice.
Your calling is uncomfortable and humbling at times, but may you seek
growth and understanding in all circumstances.
May your eyes and heart be opened to see areas you need to do better.
And may God provide you words and inspire your actions to bring about
justice in His Kingdom.

Memorable Moment:

_____

_____

_____

_____

I AM A COMFORTER

"Praise be to the God and Father of our Lord Jesus Christ, the Father of compassion and the God of all comfort, who comforts us in all our troubles, so that we can comfort those in any trouble with the comfort we ourselves receive from God."
~ 2 Corinthians 1:3-4 (NIV)

I have been forever changed by being in a professional capacity that requires me to take on the role of comforter. As I reflect, so many examples and experiences come to mind. The day begins like any other: I am waiting outside my classroom door, greeting students by name as they enter our classroom. Then, I catch the eye of one of my learners and immediately, my stomach drops. *Something isn't right.* I take a moment to sit with them and ask if everything is okay. It isn't. Then I listen – sometimes to words, sometimes only to tears. *A diagnosis, a death, an unexpected move, a lost home, a parent in prison, a new foster family. Heartbreak.*

For many of us, these experiences become a part of who we are. We often carry these concerns with us as if we have control over fixing them, because *we so desperately want to fix them*. These memories may resurface in dreams and unexpected moments, continuing to pull on our heartstrings.

Despite this very real, very difficult part of our calling, in 2 Corinthians we read how we have been equipped. I have never felt adequately trained to handle these heartbreaking moments with students, but the Apostle Paul shares this truth: *we can comfort those in any trouble with the comfort we ourselves receive from God*. Almost unexplainably, God positions us in this calling to bring Hope in seemingly hopeless situations. As we draw near to Christ's example of love and comfort, we receive what we need to comfort others. Perhaps, just being present to sit with someone and say, "I am here for you whenever you need," is the most important thing.

Today's Intention:

_____

_____

_____

_____

May the Lord Bless You and Keep You:

Today, may you be blessed by a surpassing feeling of comfort.
May the Holy Spirit give you discernment, providing words to share when
you have none, and quiet comfort when it is needed most.
In low times, may you be lifted up by the promise of your Father's presence.
And may you be a safe, comforting vessel, displaying the Hope you have
within you.

Memorable Moment:

_____

_____

_____

_____

I AM GENEROUS

"In a word, what I'm saying is, Grow up. You're kingdom subjects. Now live like it. Live out your God-created identity. Live generously and graciously toward others, the way God lives toward you."
~ Matthew 5:48 (MSG)

The way God lives toward you

Consider the generosity and grace of God. Where has God shown you unending generosity in your life? How has He blessed you in ways you could not have imagined? Where has He shown you abounding grace when you needed it the most? We may feel this when we have made it to the end of a tough day. He has led us through even the most chaotic and unexpected moments, providing an abundant supply of love, grace, and strength.

Live generously and graciously toward others

The more we dwell on God's generosity and compassion for us, the more our awareness of the blessings in life are heightened. Thankfulness becomes habitual in our lives. We have been lifted up and our perspective shifted to see the world through a lens of freedom. Our clenched fists become relaxed and open to others because of the great love God has shown us. Gradually, we *grow up* and change, displaying the marks of God's Kingdom while sharing generosity and grace with our students, colleagues, families, and community members. God gives us abundant compassion to understand others, take action, and pray fiercely.

Today's Intention:

_____

_____

_____

_____

May the Lord Bless You and Keep You:

Today, may you be filled with the Holy Spirit, inspired to live generously.
May you reflect on God's lavish gifts in your life.
May you respond to these blessings with thankfulness and praise!
May the Holy Spirit orchestrate opportunities to show generosity to others.
May these actions be rooted in Christ's love, not an obligation to provide.
And may you find freedom when you live graciously and generously.

Memorable Moment:

_____

_____

_____

_____

Part 5
I Am Creative

I AM CREATIVE

"For we are God's handiwork, created in Christ Jesus to do good work, which God prepared in advance for us to do."
~ Ephesians 2:10 (NIV)

In our field of education, we often have so many tasks and responsibilities that we may feel as if there is no room for creativity. Between lesson planning, preparing for assessments, ongoing communication, meetings, and the seemingly endless items on our to-do lists, where do we find room for imagination or innovation? Do we even have the energy to develop new ideas or share our gifts?

For a long time, I was quick to dismiss the notion I could be creative. When others would suggest I had this characteristic, I would respond, "Oh, I'm not a creative person. You should see me try to draw!" I associated creativity with the ability to design a room well or form a piece of visual art. However, I have learned that creativity is so much more diverse, and by accomplishing the tasks required of our profession, we have already developed unique skills, whether we realize it or not.

As children of God, we are fearfully and wonderfully made, designed with gifts, talents, and passions. *We are God's handiwork, created in Christ Jesus to do good work, which God prepared in advance for us to do.* You may think of more to add, but here are some examples of the creative skills we already develop and utilize as educators: problem-solving, writing a complex IEP, providing inspiration, building a classroom community, engaging an audience while reading out loud, teaching content in a relatable way, being organized, acting, speaking, listening, learning, and reflecting. With this foundation of creativity, how might we find joy in using our God-given gifts to add even more beauty to our learning spaces?

Today's Intention:

_____

_____

_____

_____

May the Lord Bless You and Keep You:
Today, may you excitedly explore the creativity God has blessed you with!
May these gifts find their way into every part of your day.
May a song, quote, or image invigorate your spirit.
May you notice the gifts of others, like little lights on a dark night.
And may you have the strength to say, "No," in some areas to make space
for cultivating creativity.

Memorable Moment:

_____

_____

_____

_____

I AM A DREAMER

"Have the audacity to keep dreaming in full color, come undone, letting hope have its way."
~ Morgan Harper Nichols [53]

What does *dreaming in full color* look like to you? Perhaps it involves exploring new ideas, perspectives, or skills. Today, we celebrate the truth that, in you, God instills hopes and dreams, aligning with His vision for our world. Our Creator designed you to be innovative, curious, passionate, and unique. In you, He built a capacity for unbelievable determination and resilience. You are capable of much more than you may allow yourself to believe.

How might you need to *come undone* in order to audaciously move forward in your life? Are there parts of your life the Holy Spirit is nudging you to shift to create some space for your full-color dreaming? Perhaps it feels as though your dreams have become forgotten, pushed aside, or diminished in value altogether. In your busy days, it may feel impossible to find the time or energy to cultivate your dreams, but ultimately you will create the space to pursue what you prioritize most.

In your journey of growing, learning, and dreaming, are you opening your hands and heart, inviting *hope to have its way?* There are far greater things ahead than any left behind if you chase them with unrelenting passion. Look forward with hope and anticipation! Beyond your wildest thoughts and imagination lie new possibilities. It can feel risky to dream big, but if you don't, you run the risk of missing out on what God has in store for you: the impact in His Kingdom, the love shared, and the communities unified and strengthened. With God, your Hope, all things are possible!

Today's Intention:

_____

_____

_____

_____

May the Lord Bless You and Keep You:
Today, may the Holy Spirit inspire full-color, beautiful dreams!
If your hopes and passions have felt distant, may you be given the
freedom to rekindle them once again.
May your soul be given fresh energy as you pray over your
God-inspired dreams.
And may you be empowered by the confidence that what God has
begun in you, He will see to fruition.

Memorable Moment:

_____

_____

_____

_____

I AM VISIONARY

"When I dare to be powerful - to use my strength in the service of my vision, it becomes less and less important whether I am afraid."
~ Audre Lorde [54]

A visionary is someone who thinks about or plans the future with imagination and wisdom. I believe God has created each of us with a unique vision, purpose, and passion for His Kingdom on earth. Imagination opens the door for limitless possibilities as we worship a limitless God. Our minds may impose restrictions on our vision, but God does not. Wisdom guides our vision into actionable steps. The Holy Spirit moves us to conduct our lives with discipline, communicate well with others, and create goals.

The reality is that it can feel daunting and lonely to pursue a vision, especially if we are not surrounded by people who are doing the same; because the moment we decide to run full force into the calling and passion God has instilled within us, we are choosing discomfort and risk. However, we are also choosing *life!* What a remarkable feeling it is when our soul and God's purpose aligns - when we have found a key part of who God has designed us to be and what we are called to do.

Therefore, we do not go alone, but stand firmly on the power and permission of Almighty God. We also trust the impactful work God is doing in the lives of those around us. As we seek community, inside or outside of our professional context, we can prayerfully welcome those God has brought (and will continue to bring) into our lives to journey with us, even if only for a season. Coming together, we use our strengths in service of God's vision for humanity. As Audre Lorde so eloquently emphasizes, *when we dare to be powerful, using our strengths in service of our vision, our fears become less and less important.*

Today's Intention:

_____

_____

_____

_____

May the Lord Bless You and Keep You:
Today, may you feel a vision developing.
May you be reminded of a passion and purpose felt long ago.
May you hear a quote, read a verse, or engage in a conversation that lights a spark once again.
May God bring others with vision into your life to walk alongside you.
And may you sense God rejoicing over you as you open your heart to His vision.

Memorable Moment:

_____

_____

_____

_____

I AM IMAGINATIVE

**"We live under wide open skies and know where we stand.
So let's not sleepwalk like these others. Let's keep our eyes
open and be smart."
~ I Thessalonians 5:5 (MSG)**

I define imagination as, "fun vulnerability." Being imaginative is almost always in pursuit of fun, play, entertainment, or creativity, but it doesn't always feel safe, particularly as we grow older. Sharing an idea or story, developed completely out of our own mind and experiences, is incredibly personal. If someone rejects it, we may feel as if they are rejecting a piece of us.

Consider our youngest children. They seem to have no hesitation sharing and acting out what they are imagining. They don't care what other people think because, in that moment, they are captivated by their ideas and the creative possibilities that are within reach. What if we embraced this lesson from our children?

As our reflection verse reminds us, *we live under wide open skies and know where we stand.* God designed us in His image with His creative Spirit. Imagination invites us to ask: *What if?*
If we are teachers of younger children especially, we are beckoned into their worlds, captivated by the ridiculous, the silly, the fantastical, and the unorganized parts of our existence. It welcomes us into a space to inspire learners of all ages to write *that* story, sing *that* song, and try *that* experiment. Because, without our imaginations, what would our world look like?

Today's Intention:

_____

_____

_____

_____

May the Lord Bless You and Keep You:

May your mind come alive in imagination today.
May you risk sharing laughter and vulnerability as you encourage,
create, and learn.
May you become more aware of how the Holy Spirit inspires ideas.
And in the midst of the wide-open skies, may you always know where
you stand.

Memorable Moment:

_____

_____

_____

_____

I AM A RISK-TAKER

**"Sameness breeds more sameness until you make a
thoughtful effort to counteract it."
~ Michelle Obama** [55]

When I first read this quote by Michelle Obama in her book,
"Becoming," I immediately thought about our public school system.
Sameness. However, experienced teachers have told me teaching is not
what it used to be. Something has shifted. Somehow, the world has
more needs which we, as educators and caregivers, are being asked to
fill. So, it seems as if not all is the same. Our students are changing. Our
society is moving forward in new and exciting ways, and in grieving
ways as well.

We find our situations conflicting when our students and their needs
are changing, but our systems and practices are not. When we step
into our learning spaces and see very little progress for our students,
teachers, and leadership, we must ask if enough thoughtful effort has
been made to address these growing responsibilities and challenges. I
do not believe our God is a passive, wait-for-it-to-happen God.

In His journey on earth, Jesus Christ was a risk-taker – perhaps the
boldest risk-taker to ever walk the earth. I believe this is evidenced in
two ways. First, He challenged the "sameness." He counteracted norms
of His societal environment regarding how to treat others and how to
achieve greatness. Secondly, He was unapologetically committed to
His calling. God's Son was sent to demonstrate His unconditional love
to His creation. He journeyed while telling stories - at times
uncomfortable stories - and performing miracles by connecting
personally with the people around Him. We are called to follow His
example in our respective positions by making a thoughtful effort for
how to counteract systems and practices that go against God's vision
for our children, families, and communities.

Today's Intention:

_____

_____

_____

_____

May the Lord Bless You and Keep You:

Today, may you accept the invitation to be the hands and feet of Christ.
May you risk feeling uncomfortable in order to reap great outcomes in
God's Kingdom.
May the Holy Spirit protect you from becoming complacent in your
personal and professional life.
And may you be emboldened to live out the great calling God has entrusted
to you.

Memorable Moment:

_____

_____

_____

_____

I AM INSPIRED

"But it is God whose power made the earth, whose wisdom gave shape to the world, who crafted the cosmos."
~ Jeremiah 10:12 (MSG)

When my motivation, or passionate energy, is fading, I have found it helpful to reflect on who or what inspires me, and to write this down as a list. Then, I intentionally plan how I will involve these people and activities in my own life. It seems so simple, but in all the busyness, sometimes I forget to play my favorite song or catch up with a close friend, for example. So today, let's try this practice together:

Who inspires you?
Who can you sit with, conversing for hours, and leave feeling uplifted?
Who do you have "real talks" with - discussions that are vulnerable and sometimes challenging?
Who do you look up to, and why?

What inspires you?
What books, movies, songs, podcasts, or videos bring energy to your heart?
Where do you go to feel inspired?
What hobbies or activities build you up and cultivate creativity?
How does your faith inspire you?

In Jeremiah, we read how God's power, wisdom, and creativity brought our beautiful world into being. This same God created you. And just think of it - the same Inspiration that formed planets, stars, and galaxies inspires you in your calling every day.

Today's Intention:

_____

_____

_____

_____

May the Lord Bless You and Keep You:
Today, may you dwell on the power and imagination of our Creator, and be inspired!
May God shape your day, guiding your learning opportunities and relationship building.
May the Holy Spirit bless you with wisdom, new ideas, and creative pathways.
And may this inspiration be contagious, lighting the way for others to be inspired.

Memorable Moment:

_____

_____

_____

_____

I AM BOLD

"To live a creative life, we must lose our fear of being wrong."
~ Joseph Chilton Pearce [56]

What hinders creativity and action? Are we hesitant to boldly embrace a creative life because we fear failure, hold worries of disappointing others, or have concerns about our image and how others will perceive us? Perhaps, we have heard messages such as, "Play it safe," or, "Don't rock the boat," which leave us feeling as if boldness is selfish, extravagant, or disruptive. To be bold means to take risks with confidence and courage. Does it seem incongruous that the place of vulnerable creativity is also where we demonstrate confidence and courage? How do we let go of our fear of being wrong?

I wonder if Jesus weighed the risks He was taking in His ministry. Did He ever have fears or hesitations? I do not know the answer, but we do know He did not allow those to hinder Him from embracing opportunities to share the message of God's love and generosity. Jesus healed lepers, going against the societal norms and practices of remaining clean. He refused to condemn a woman caught in adultery, challenging how people perceived and judged one another. Our Teacher risked His life, lost His life, and had His life restored, so we might live free from the power of sin. What a bold example to follow!

How do we express boldness, letting go of the fear of being wrong? Perhaps, we begin overcoming this fear with the realization of what opportunities could be missed if we do not act boldly. Like Jesus, we recognize: God has placed paths in front of us, and He has designed us with gifts and abilities to display His glory. So we take risks, confident in the plans God has for us and encouraged by the One who became bold for us.

Today's Intention:

_____

_____

_____

_____

May the Lord Bless You and Keep You:

Today, may you acknowledge with gratitude the gifts God has instilled within you.

May you have supernatural confidence and courage in the One who called you to this work.

May you find the freedom and conviction to take risks in areas God is leading you to stretch.

And may the Holy Spirit invigorate your heart with boldness for your students and community.

Memorable Moment:

_____

_____

_____

_____

I AM WANDERING

"Unless the Lord builds the house, the builders labor in vain. Unless the Lord watches over the city, the guards stand watch in vain. In vain you rise early and stay up late, toiling for food to eat — for he grants sleep to those he loves."
~ Psalm 127:1-2 (NIV)

I wonder how many of us resonate with these habits: staying awake, rising early, going to bed late, eating out of anxiousness, and the list goes on. One thing I learned toward the end of my first year as a teacher is the to-do lists never actually end. I wish there would have been a course in my collegiate training to inform me of this sooner because I made, and still make, well-intended lists in vain. As teachers, it feels like there is always more we can do: more creative approaches, more communication with families, more feedback to students, or more support for our colleagues. How do we balance it all?

Our reflection verses from Psalms provide comfort. They remind us we can work all day and night, but if God is not directing our focus, we will be wandering. What if instead of diving headfirst into our lesson plans, we paused for a moment to open our hearts to God, giving Him space to direct our instruction based on what students will need to hear, know, and do? What if instead of frantically hustling into Monday, we intentionally entrusted the week into God's hands, and then moved on to the next thing? I wonder how our perspectives might change.

Unless the Lord builds the house, the builders labor in vain. We could put these words into our own experiences by reflecting, *Unless the Lord builds our classroom community, facilitates our learning, and strengthens relationships, the teachers labor in vain.* As we entrust our circumstances to God, we will be more focused and peaceful on our journeys.

Today's Intention:

_____

_____

_____

_____

May the Lord Bless You and Keep You:

As you enter the day, mind racing with the tasks ahead, may you trust God's wisdom and vision.

Where your mind and heart feel wandering, may Jesus draw you close to His love.

May you believe in the intervention of His Spirit, however unique and subtle it may be.

May your ears be in tune with His voice over your day.

Memorable Moment:

_____

_____

_____

_____

I AM AUTHENTIC

**"We have different gifts,
according to the grace given to each of us."
~ Romans 12:6a (NIV)**

I'd like to structure our time together differently today. My attempt to write a reflection focused on your authenticity would likely feel ineffective. You know you best. So today, I invite you to write our reflection by filling in words that describe you. As you think of and name pieces of yourself, let us thank God for creating you in intricate detail and for the gifts He has given you.

I am _____ .

I am _____ .

I am _____ .

I am _____ .

I am _____ .

The word, "authentic," means to be of undisputed origin. Praise be to God for creating you exactly as you are. He has designed you in His image out of His love, giving you undisputed origin.

Praise be to Jesus Christ for how He leads you in using your very presence to bless the world. While on the earth, His origin was disputed many times; however, Jesus was grounded in His identity as God's Son.

Praise be to the Holy Spirit for guiding you in how to use your gifts to bless the lives of others.

Today's Intention:

_____

_____

_____

_____

May the Lord Bless You and Keep You:

May the Holy Spirit remind you of your undisputed origin as a child of God. May you embrace the qualities and quirks that make you authentically you. May God orchestrate opportunities for you to use your gifts to bless others. Today, in your listening and speaking, your doing and resting, may you show up as your truest self.

Memorable Moment:

_____

_____

_____

_____

I AM SIMPLE

**"Let me give you a new command:
Love one another. In the same way I loved you, you love one
another. This is how everyone will recognize that you are my
disciples - when they see the love you have for each other."
~ John 13:34-35 (MSG)**

Our reflection verses today highlight an impactful moment in Jesus' ministry. Jesus had just finished washing His disciples' feet, a surprising demonstration of humility and service. After this, He alludes to the events which will soon unfold, exposing the betrayal of their companion, Judas, who then abruptly departs, leaving lingering questions with the remaining disciples. Can we imagine the nervous confusion building in that "Last Supper" room? All of this was leading up to the most chaotic, emotionally taxing time in Jesus' ministry. Yet, this is when Jesus chooses to focus on the most important thing. In an instant, He simplifies everything for His friends: *Love one another.*

Sometimes, we may inadvertently create obstacles in our own path of simplicity. It is easy and habitual to get caught up in the details of life. We attempt to balance so many responsibilities, find answers to questions, and solve problems relying on our own strength. We may experience seasons when we feel overwhelmed and are left with lingering questions for God and His plan. Earlier in this chapter, Jesus told Peter, "You don't understand now what I'm doing, but it will be clear enough to you later" (John 13:7 MSG). Perhaps this is a reminder we need to hear today as well.

Jesus simplifies everything for us when He says: *Love one another.* He does not dismiss or condemn our distracted efforts. He simply invites a different way of thinking: the freedom to love the person in front of us, next to us, or across the world from us. On certain days, we may need to hear permission to simply and extravagantly love the way Christ loves us. *This is how everyone will recognize we are His disciples - when we love one another.*

Today's Intention:

_____

_____

_____

_____

May the Lord Bless You and Keep You:

Today, may you feel Jesus' love for you in a personal way.
May this Love enter into every part of who you are, simplifying your
words and actions.
May the Holy Spirit fill your mind with clarity, focusing on the most
important purpose:
May you love one another.

Memorable Moment:

_____

_____

_____

_____

I AM COMPLEX

I want you woven into a tapestry of love, in touch with everything there is to know of God. Then you will have minds confident and at rest, focused on Christ, God's great mystery. All the richest treasures of wisdom and knowledge are embedded in that mystery and nowhere else. And we've been shown the mystery!
~ Colossians 2:2-3 (MSG)

In our previous reflection, we focused on the theme of simplicity, anchoring our purpose on loving one another. Today, we explore the mystery and complexity of our lives. We are dynamic, multi-faceted human beings. We each have our own unique characteristics and quirks, often striving to find the perfect balance between our personal and professional lives. At times, complexity can feel scattered, disoriented, and unorganized. Whether we feel complex individually or as a school community, we may find ourselves searching for unity and clarity, the simplicity of Love once again.

"Complex," is a fascinating word which can be used as a noun, adjective, and even a verb in some cases. From its Latin roots, complex means to join, unite, entwine around, or embrace. *Plexus*, part of this root, means "intricately woven." Embedded in the origins of complexity, we find the simplicity of unification. We are reminded that in God, there is a mystery we do not fully see. And yet in all things, He is working to *weave us into a tapestry of love*.

When creating a tapestry, the weavers often intertwine the threads from behind the developing tapestry, not seeing the full picture from its frontal view. In front of the tapestry, there is a large mirror reflecting the image forming on the front, as well as the original design, which is hung behind the working weavers. When the weavers maintain their focus on the mirror, they can see the design reflected onto the threads they are weaving. Similarly in our lives of faith, "Now we see only a reflection as in a mirror; then we shall see face to face. Now I know in part; then I shall know fully, even as I am fully known" (1 Corinthians 13:12 NIV).

Today's Intention:

_____

_____

_____

_____

May the Lord Bless You and Keep You:
Today, may you feel embraced by the unconditional love of God.
May you feel truly known by your Heavenly Comforter.
May the Holy Spirit weave you into the rich tapestry of love, in touch with everything there is to know about God.
In the complexities and uncertainties, may your mind be confident and at rest, focused on Christ.

Memorable Moment:

_____

_____

_____

_____

I AM UNIQUE

"Two roads diverged in a wood, and I - I took the one less traveled by, And that has made all the difference."
~ Robert Frost [57]

I am unique.

I see the world in a way not quite like anyone else.

I see opportunities where some find failure.

And that has made all the difference.

I am too energetic for some and have too little gumption for others.

I am proactive, and I am spontaneous.

I develop hobbies and interests that display a part of me.

And that has made all the difference.

Sometimes, my dreams and passions are too bold to share,

But I keep them inside my heart.

I meditate on them at night, this urging God has placed in me.

I am unique.

And that has made all the difference.

Today's Intention:

_____

_____

_____

_____

May the Lord Bless You and Keep You:

You are unique, created in the image of our Heavenly Father.
May you see your mannerisms and style in a new light today.
May you not conform to the patterns of this world, but live in
transformation.
With God's grace and direction, may you take the road less traveled by,
making the difference for others to embrace their unique gifts and abilities.

Memorable Moment:

_____

_____

_____

_____

I AM A LEARNER

"A teacher who loves learning earns the right and the ability to help others learn."
~ Ruth Beechick [58]

A truly special area of our calling is engaging in ongoing learning as we grow as educators. Whether we are researching U.S. History to support the outlined standards or are developing our pedagogical and instructional craft, we can feel refreshed when we are learning. However, here we also find the challenge. Teaching, coaching, and the exploration it requires is incredibly exhausting. Channeling the core part of us that loves learning may feel more difficult as the school year progresses. I believe God has designed our minds in a way to enjoy learning and growing. It is healthy for us.

So how do we incorporate this practice into our lives when we feel overwhelmed? Here are a few ideas that have worked for me. First, identify the things that bring you life. Explore more about these topics by finding podcasts, websites, books, blogs, or documentaries focused on these areas. You could delve into these resources on your commute, while folding laundry, or in another way that works for you. Next, incorporate an attitude of learning and exploration with your students. Creating an atmosphere for questions and discoveries invites excitement into your learning space.

When we intentionally take small steps to learn, new life is inspired. Gaining knowledge is like filling our appetites for the nourishment that feeds our soul. Once we taste the opportunity of increased potential - once our eyes are opened to a world beyond our limited perspective - we can't help but seek after more!

Today's Intention:

_____

_____

_____

_____

May the Lord Bless You and Keep You:
Today, may you feel inspired to learn something new!
May God bring to mind new ideas and curiosities.
_May the Holy Spirit defend against anything that hinders you from
positive growth._
_And may God open up new possibilities for you and those around
you in your learning adventure!_

Memorable Moment:

_____

_____

_____

_____

I AM VIBRANT

"You're here to be light, bringing out the God-colors in the world."
~ Matthew 5:14 (MSG)

Imagine a room filled with various items, each in its own beautiful color. There are soft pinks and royal blues. In this room, we find the boldest yellow and the kindest purple. In an awe-inspiring kaleidoscope, reds, greens, browns, oranges and every shade in between is represented, each with its unique subtleties and designs.

This room is truly magical, but there is one problem: There is no light. Anyone who takes a step in this space will only see darkness and emptiness. If only someone would bring in a light or throw back the curtains to let the natural light into the room. All of this brightness is waiting to be seen; it just needs the proper lighting.

Consider the analogy from our reflection verse in Matthew's Gospel. Our call is to be that source of light in the places we work and serve. Every student is created in the image of God, and therefore holds God-colors in them. They have unique strengths, abilities, and interests. Our Heavenly Creator designed them this way, but many have never had someone enter the darkness long enough to illuminate their God-colors. We have this opportunity today.

Today's Intention:

_____

_____

_____

_____

May the Lord Bless You and Keep You:
Today, may you be a vibrant light.
You have traveled through much darkness, bringing Light with you along the way.
May your light shine brightly, illuminating the gifts of your students and colleagues.
May others see themselves in a new way because of your searching and believing.
And may your God-colors bring inspiration and positive change to your community.

Memorable Moment:

_____

_____

_____

_____

I AM OBSERVANT

"It is not our differences that divide us. It is our inability to recognize, accept, and celebrate those differences."
~ Audre Lorde [59]

It takes a special skill to be observant, to scan around your learning space and not just look, but *see*. Observation is a key component of our calling in education. Consider this scenario:

It's a busy, energetic day in your classroom. After circulating around the room answering questions and providing support, you pause for a moment to catch your breath. In those few seconds, you watch. You watch everything happening around you. There are students who may need another reminder of the expected task. You see a student helping another, and it occurs to you these students aren't friends, nor have they previously interacted with each other; and yet, they are supporting each other. You listen to a child tell a joke they just made up. You overhear a teenager quietly confide to a friend about a difficult situation at home. When you pause to observe for those few moments, your eyes and heart are opened a little wider.

Taking the time to reflect on our surroundings is critical. It helps us tune into our learning space, appreciate the blessings we have been given, and become aware of barriers we might not have noticed. It also reminds us that our students are *human*, with complex emotions and experiences. Being observant means recognizing the similarities and differences in our learning community and identifying how these nuances strengthen our space. We embrace and celebrate our unique gifts which God has designed within each person, all while acknowledging we are made in our Creator's image, sharing the same origin.

Today's Intention:

_____

_____

_____

_____

May the Lord Bless You and Keep You:

Today, may the Holy Spirit open your eyes and ears to be in tune with God's perspective.
May you view those around you through His lens, with unconditional love and genuine curiosity.
May your observations lead to new ideas for coaching, conversation, and connection.
And may truths of acceptance and celebration be echoed in your midst.

Memorable Moment:

_____

_____

_____

_____

I AM AN AWAKENER

"I am not a teacher, but an awakener."
~ Robert Frost [60]

There is something so comforting about a warm fire. It brings me back to cool summer nights, roasting marshmallows over a crackling fire, or cold winter mornings with snow falling and everyone congregating around the hearth. Fire possesses underlying purposes, bringing people together to experience joy and nourishment.

Fire has the capacity for both comfort and power. It begins with a simple spark. Consider a match in a matchbox. It has so much potential, but nothing will happen until someone first takes action. One must pick up the box and open it carefully to select a match. Then a swift, coordinated swipe of the match to the side of the box is required to bring a spark to life. From here, another action needs to be taken: movement, transporting the lit match to the object needing to experience a spark next. From a simple spark comes limitless potential if intentional action is taken.

Consider how the Holy Spirit awakens passion and purpose in our lives, like a simple spark igniting into something greater. We are both comforted and empowered by this internal intervention. As teachers, we have the honor and responsibility of awakening possibility within our students as well. Perhaps, even one movement - an intentional question or thoughtful comment - will ignite ideas and positive beliefs about themselves. When the mind, body, and spirit experience awakening, then comfort, power, and adventure are illuminated.

Today's Intention:

_____

_____

_____

_____

May the Lord Bless You and Keep You:
May God fill your spirit with a sense of adventure!
May you be reminded of what sets your soul on fire.
As you step into your learning space, may you have eyes to see those
who are missing their spark.
May the Holy Spirit work through you to awaken the sparks of
interest, creativity, and zest in others.

Memorable Moment:

_____

_____

_____

_____

I AM A MOTIVATOR

"The reason I love teaching, it's like being a miner. I find all these undiscovered jewels and, with the right motivation, they're amazed at what they can do. I have to show them their capability."
~ Rafe Esquith [61]

Mining for jewels and precious metals is a fascinating process. There are many different methods used to locate and extract these special materials. First, a space is chosen where miners will either break into the earth through tunnels and shafts, or slowly dig down deep into a large open place. Then, the miners search these areas with various tools and technologies. When a jewel is found, it can be removed using a variety of strategies: pry bars, picks, shovels, drilling, or even explosives! The method of release depends on the jewel and its status in the dirt and rock.

The work miners do feels similar to how Jesus searches for and pulls us out of the rubble using diverse approaches. He is the Shepherd who leaves the ninety-nine to look for the one lost sheep. He is the Healer who bends down to provide comfort to the sick, beginning by comforting their souls and then their physical bodies. He is the Teacher who recognizes the questions, strengths, and passions of His followers, and then motivates them to live out their calling.

In our reflection quote today, teaching is compared to the practice of mining, always on the lookout for undiscovered jewels. Through intentional observation, key questioning, and a creative mind, we identify the amazing God-given gifts our students possess. Then we use varying methods and approaches to unearth their potential, motivating them to live out their capabilities in amazing ways. Perhaps we use a "pick," slowly reminding students of their worth, belonging, and strength. For others, it may be an "explosive" moment of excitement when breakthrough occurs! Our students become motivated because someone sees them, believes in them, and empowers them for who they are.

Today's Intention:

_____

_____

_____

_____

May the Lord Bless You and Keep You:

Today, may you enter your space of learning as a miner, searching for undiscovered jewels.

May your heart fill with excitement as you seek opportunities that are waiting to be explored.

May the Holy Spirit motivate your words and actions as you encourage those around you.

And may your students feel treasured for exactly who God has created them to be.

Memorable Moment:

_____

_____

_____

_____

I AM ADAPTIVE

"Teaching is a wonderful way to learn."
~ Carol Dweck [62]

To adapt Carol Dweck's quote in my own way, "Teaching is an invitation to learn." When we engage in wholehearted learning, we come to realize more about the world around us by gaining information and developing understanding. Any time our awareness and experiences are widening, adaptation will take place because we are adjusting to new conditions in our mind, body, and spirit.

The relationship between teaching and learning is intimately connected. Effective teaching is adaptive teaching, and we will only be able to adapt if and when we are receptive to learning. Consider all the authentic ways we adjust our plans on a daily basis. A lesson may not go quite as planned. Perhaps the school assembly or mandated fire drill was rescheduled, shifting how the day will progress. The examples continue as we identify that we are incredibly adaptive professionals!

We learn as we go, strengthening our understanding as we make mistakes and encounter challenges. The openness to adjust to new conditions requires observation, continual learning, and action. The Holy Spirit walks alongside us, adapting our perspective so we may identify new opportunities and strengthen already effective routines. As we remain focused on God's calling to be present for our students, we will notice how He has been elevating voices in our learning spaces. We see approaches and hear perspectives which provide chances to adapt the content we are teaching. This creates powerful instruction and learning!

Today's Intention:

_____

_____

_____

_____

May the Lord Bless You and Keep You:

Today, may God strengthen your community of learners.
May you enjoy seeking new, fresh methods of learning.
May the Holy Spirit give you wisdom, understanding, and creativity in
your craft.
May you approach your day with curiosity, inviting opportunities for
adaptation and growth.
And may unity and discovery unfold before your eyes.

Memorable Moment:

_____

_____

_____

_____

I AM LIGHTHEARTED

"Are you worsted in a fight? Laugh it off.
Are you cheated of your right? Laugh it off.
Don't make tragedy out of trifles,
Don't shoot butterflies with rifles - Laugh it off.
Does your work get into kinks? Laugh it off.
Are you near all sorts of brinks? Laugh it off.
If it's sanity you're after, there's no recipe like laughter
Laugh it off."
~ Henry Rutherford Elliot [63]

Life is about balance. Teaching is about balance. There are serious and sensitive moments, but there are also times when a healthy course of action may be laughter and a lighthearted spirit. I imagine God watching our students with amusement and pleasure, enjoying their wit, quirkiness, and youthfulness. There is a freedom that emerges when we are able to laugh about the goofy things or the silly mix-ups.

When we build trusting relationships and rapport with our students, we create a safe space to share humor. Remember, some of our students live in a lighthearted environment at home, where joking feels safe and inclusive. They may feel comfortable in a setting where this is a part of the atmosphere in a respectful way. When we entrust our words and actions to God, I believe the Holy Spirit intervenes on our behalf, directing us in appropriate ways to handle our daily circumstances.

We do not need to fear embracing a lighthearted approach. Not everything needs to be taken too seriously or too personally. We are in much more control of our attitude and mood than we often realize. Let's explore creating a space where we clear our mind of negative clutter and make room for the delight and laughter that life brings.

Today's Intention:

_____

_____

_____

_____

May the Lord Bless You and Keep You:

Today, may the Holy Spirit widen your awareness of the blessing of lighthearted moments.
May you seize opportunities to smile and laugh.
May joy radiate from your learning space.
When there is a bump in the road, may you find the ease to roll right along.
And may God give you His lens of love, admiration, and joy as you interact with your students.

Memorable Moment:

_____

_____

_____

_____

I AM GIFTED

"Then let us all do what is right, strive with all our might toward the unattainable, develop as fully as we can the gifts God has given us, and never stop learning."
~ Ludwig Van Beethoven [64]

...strive with all our might toward the unattainable...

It feels implausible, doesn't it - striving with all our might toward what is unreachable? We may think: *Who am I to try to achieve this great goal? It's impossible.* In our questioning, we are reminded that with God, all things are possible! Jesus defeated the word, "unattainable," when He was raised from the dead to demonstrate God's love for us. Let us also challenge the unattainable perceptions in our mind, so we may focus on what God has named possible.

...develop as fully as we can the gifts God has given us...

God has given us incredible gifts of all kinds. We begin in awareness of what these gifts are. Pause for a moment to think about the dreams, interests, passions, and abilities God has instilled in you. Reflect also on all the ways God has gifted you to serve your family, students, and community. It is our responsibility and joy to steward these gifts well for His glory.

...and never stop learning.

This is the key. Our gifts strengthen and gain momentum as we expose them to ideas, perspectives, and skills. A musician's gift would be lovely, yet limited, if they only learned and perfected one song. A carpenter's gift would be efficient, yet monotonous, if they only created the same chair over and over again. We grow in and through our gift, taking pride in new heights achieved, and setting sights for higher.

In Beethoven's words, *this is what is right.*

Today's Intention:

_____

_____

_____

_____

May the Lord Bless You and Keep You:

*Today, as you take time to reflect on God's design for your life, may
you reflect and be thankful for the gifts He has given you.
May you courageously step forward to pursue what feels unattainable,
confident that God has made all things possible through Jesus Christ.
May the Holy Spirit empower you into action, strengthening and using
your gifts for God's purposes.*

Memorable Moment:

_____

_____

_____

_____

I AM VERSATILE

"And [the Lord] has filled him with the Spirit of God, with wisdom, with understanding, with knowledge, and with all kinds of skills."
~ Exodus 35:31 (NIV)

Let's consider our versatility for a moment. In our daily responsibilities, think about how often we adapt to multiple objectives, roles, and activities. For many of us, this is all day, every day! We journey through the day, ebbing and flowing, moving from one expectation to another. For example, we may begin the day facilitating a staff meeting. Then we adapt to the role of instructional designer as we plan our upcoming lessons. Quickly, we step into our "counseling shoes" as we comfort a struggling student. This could all happen within an hour with the rest of the day still in front of us. There is no denying it: We have been gifted with versatile abilities!

As we explore versatility, let's build some context around today's reflection verse. Moses was leading an offering before God. Out of praise and gratitude for God's provision in their lives, many people were symbolically laying down their prized possessions on an altar. Others also came near and offered their gifts and abilities to the service of God. Some of these gifts are described as: *being filled with the Spirit of God, wisdom, understanding, knowledge, and all other kinds of skills.*

When we answered our call to the classroom, did we realize we were stepping near to the altar of God, offering our many skills and abilities? When our Heavenly Designer formed us, He built into us the capacity to be versatile, to adapt to various purposes, roles, and activities. God first gave us these gifts as a blessing, and now we have the honor and privilege of using these gifts to bless His Kingdom.

Today's Intention:

_____

_____

_____

_____

May the Lord Bless You and Keep You:

Today, may your space of learning feel like the altar of God: a place to bring your versatile gifts and abilities in service and praise to Him. As you navigate the many responsibilities before you, may you be filled with the Spirit of God.
May you have wisdom, understanding, and knowledge.
And may you be blessed with skills of all kinds as you bless those around you.

Memorable Moment:

_____

_____

_____

_____

I AM AN ARTIST

"The teacher must be an actor, an artist, passionately in love with his work."
~ Anton Chekhov [65]

Creatives have no limits.
It is the open-minded, limitless thinkers among us
Who illuminate the world.
One sees an image and curiosity grows,
Dozens of questions filling the mind.
Another hears a song,
And suddenly melodies of unifying possibility emerge!
An athlete, in love with the sport,
Shows strength of skill and strategy.
A piece of writing may spur surprising outcomes
In the mind and soul of the reader.
"The show must go on!" cry the faithful, fervent actors
Who bring to the world stories, new and old.

In Jesus Christ, we have no limits.
Inspired by our Creator,
We are diverse, unique, and gifted with power.
Made in the image of God, we are also intimately connected.
We are teachers:
Actors, performers, artists, athletes, speakers, and creators.
Daily, we choose to be passionately in love with this work,
To examine the intricacies,
And to sketch bold beauty into our spaces of learning.
On the days when passion fades,
We look to our Heavenly Artist and dwell in His inspiration.

Today's Intention:

_____

_____

_____

_____

May the Lord Bless You and Keep You:

As this day begins, may you observe your environment for signs of God's inspiration.

May colors look brighter and textures feel compelling, as you pause in awe of our Heavenly Artist.

May you embrace education as your art and specialty, passionately in love with this work.

May the Holy Spirit expose the pieces of yourself that so desperately crave to display their potential.

May your artistry inspire creativity and confidence all around you.

Memorable Moment:

_____

_____

_____

_____

I AM A SPEAKER

"When you talk to them, put all your love and sweetness into your words - or rather ask Jesus to speak through you."
~ Mother Teresa [66]

A phrase used often in my classroom is: "Words have the power to build up or tear down. Choose carefully how you use them." At times, I wonder who benefits more from this reminder: my students or myself. What we say and how we express our words, holds a tremendous amount of potential impact. Words are powerful because, once said, they are unretractable.

Our days are filled with words: seemingly constant voices from our students, conversations with colleagues, and feedback from families. Then we add our words of instruction, coaching, and counseling. Speaking and listening to words can become overwhelming, and in the midst of all of this, we are expected to *put all our love and sweetness into our words?*

Ask Jesus to speak through you. When our capacity for love, generosity, and grace in our words is decreasing, this is the most important time to pause before we speak. The Holy Spirit can act as a buffer or filter if we foster the intentional practice of seeking God in the challenging moments. Sometimes, less is more. Perhaps, we begin with listening until we feel the discernment to say what truly needs to be heard. When we speak, we express words that build up, even during difficult conversations. We trust the Holy Spirit to intervene in moments when we feel close to "tearing down." God has designed our speech to have the potential for positive, powerful outcomes; therefore, we draw on His words to provide direction.

Today's Intention:

_____

_____

_____

_____

May the Lord Bless You and Keep You:
May your words hold great power and encouragement.
May your uplifting comments remain in the hearts and minds of your
students forever.
May God use your voice to change someone's perspective today.
May you reflect on what you say and the impact of others' words in
your own life.
May you speak Life into this dark world.

Memorable Moment:

_____

_____

_____

_____

I AM A WRITER

"You can make anything by writing."
~ C.S. Lewis [67]

When I was around seven years old, my oldest sister gave me a small journal. She was away at college and told me I could write to her in this journal and she would read it whenever she came home to visit. For the next several years, I wrote my ideas in that little book (mostly including commentary on the food I ate that day or the score of the Minnesota Twins baseball game). Despite its mediocre beginnings, the habit of pausing and reflecting on my day had been built into the fibers of my development. I continued the practice of journaling throughout middle and high school, navigating my shifting feelings and questions. Now, I write to process my thinking, relationships, faith, and goals.

Whether you consider yourself a writer or not, there is a lot of power in documenting your thoughts, emotions, and reflections. You are giving the innermost part of your identity room on a page. You have validity and a voice. As C.S. Lewis articulates, *you can make anything by writing*. Words hold power, and the action of putting them to print invites time to sit with these words. It means our feelings and opinions are more than just any other fleeting thought that enters and quickly leaves. Our stories, ideas, and imagination have the space to breathe and explore!

Consider the impact and influence of the Holy stories and poems we read in the Bible. From these accounts, we are inspired, uplifted, and identified. We may read experiences or emotions we can relate to, strengthening our faith as we grow our awareness that God understands us deeply. Our Author created us with stories to share, insights to record, and legacies to leave. A consistent practice of writing can enrich our lives in ways that may catch us by surprise!

Today's Intention:

_____

_____

_____

_____

May the Lord Bless You and Keep You:
Today, may you be empowered as a writer.
May you embrace the power of your words and steward this potential
· to glorify God.
May the act of writing bring relief and clarity in a wandering time.
May your reflections draw you closer to your Author and to your soul.
As you have been inspired, may you inspire others to share their
voices through the pen or keyboard.

Memorable Moment:

_____

_____

_____

_____

I AM PLAYFUL

"Play is often talked about as if it were a relief from some serious learning. But for children, play is serious learning. Play is really the work of childhood."
~ Fred Rogers [68]

When was the last time you played? Can you envision it in your mind? Take a moment to put yourself in that space. What feelings did you have? Did you laugh? Did you feel comfortable, safe, adventurous, or free? Are you wishing you could go back to that moment right now?

Was the scene you just envisioned a time you played in your classroom? If not, have you ever done that before? I believe play is really for all ages. When we play in our schools and places of learning, it engages our memory and positive feelings associated with that environment. Some of my sweetest moments as a teacher have been when students ask me to play with them, and I pause what I'm doing to join in the fun. Or sometimes, I embrace my silly side and teach the math lesson as if I were announcing a baseball game, celebrating a "home run" when a student solves a question, and announcing a "foul ball" when we need to try again. When I invite a playful spirit, all of a sudden, the students feel it too. We're exploring new information *and* playing at the same time. Perhaps, learning was always meant to be that way.

Regardless of the age group you teach, how can you incorporate play and laughter into your space? What fun, interesting activities can be embedded in any grade level? If you haven't explored this area too much, consider this your invitation! Think of those special areas that bring joy to your heart and share them with your students. It is okay if it feels vulnerable at first. You can start by noticing how your students are already engaging in their form of play, *the work of childhood*. You are blessed to work with children and young adults every day. Isn't this one of the best parts of our calling?

Today's Intention:

_____

_____

_____

_____

May the Lord Bless You and Keep You:

May you awaken a spirit of playful adventure in your learning space.
May you watch and listen for how your students are navigating life in their own unique ways.
May you find the freedom to laugh with your students, and to make time for play in your day.
May the Holy Spirit bring to mind creative ways to explore and learn with your students.
And may you have fun!

Memorable Moment:

_____

_____

_____

_____

I AM A PERFORMER

"Do not neglect your gift, which was given you through prophecy when the body of elders laid their hands on you."
~ 1 Timothy 4:14 (NIV)

To teach is to perform,
Capturing the attention of toddlers and teenagers,
Engaging an audience through words and pictures,
An artist in their element.

Voice raised and voice lowered,
Inviting voices from the crowd to add meaning.
Questions asked and questions answered;
Some remain a mystery, igniting curiosity for future generations.

Experimentation enlivening the environment;
Beakers and test tubes bubble with excitement,
As the dance of exploration begins.
The costume: a white lab coat.
Our future scientists,
Drawn into the rhythms of hypotheses and theories:
Limitless possibilities.

So pull back the curtain of your classroom!
Take the stage, educators!
It is time to own your craft,
Delivering facts and figures with vigor!
For the magic of an unforgettable performance
Leaves a legacy for years to come.

Today's Intention:

_____

_____

_____

_____

May the Lord Bless You and Keep You:
May you take pride in your professional field.
May you be reminded of what invited you into education.
May you be filled with creativity and confidence as you go about your daily tasks.
May they feel a little less normal today.
And may God inspire your heart to have fun and love what you do.

Memorable Moment:

_____

_____

_____

_____

I AM INNOVATIVE

"It is very hard to have ideas. It's very hard to put yourself out there, it's very hard to be vulnerable, but those people who do that are the dreamers, the thinkers and the creators. They are the magic people of the world."
~ Amy Poehler [69]

I love the way the word, "innovative," sounds. When I hear it, it feels gritty, powerful, conceptual, and full of action. I imagine someone with messy hair, holding a mug of extra strong coffee, getting to work, and finding solutions to problems. Innovation feels raw, authentic, and purposeful.

Innovative means to introduce new ideas, while demonstrating original and creative thinking. New ideas are born out of current circumstances. An innovator asks: *What is already working effectively? What can be adjusted to promote stronger outcomes? Whose voice needs to be invited to the conversation?* Innovation is identifying a common goal and dreaming and doing until one goal is met, and the next target is established.

Brainstorming and taking action on solutions for our current challenges can feel like an intense obligation. However, we rest in the reality that we are not burdened, but emboldened to innovate. God invites us to dream of what could be: free from the need to commend or condemn what has been the reality thus far. We are not hopeless or helpless when we follow God's leading because we rely on the Holy Spirit for grace and guidance. We are equipped to be *dreamers, thinkers, and creators,* boldly moving forward in God's wisdom and calling.

Today's Intention:

_____

_____

_____

_____

May the Lord Bless You and Keep You:

Today, may you feel emboldened to innovate!
May you be surrounded by others who are grounded in our purpose.
May the Holy Spirit inspire you with questions, ideas, and wisdom.
May Jesus be with you and lead you as you dream and create, giving Him all the glory.

Memorable Moment:

_____

_____

_____

_____

I AM DETERMINED

"But Ruth replied, 'Don't urge me to leave you or to turn back from you. Where you go I will go, and where you stay I will stay. Your people will be my people and your God my God.' ...When Naomi realized that Ruth was determined to go with her, she stopped urging her."
~ Ruth 1:16,18 (NIV)

I wonder if Ruth felt a passionate calling. After losing her husband, her support system, and the future she had envisioned, what caused her to be so determined to remain with Naomi, her mother-in-law? We can infer Ruth was empathetic, loving, and strong; however, I think these attributes only scratch the surface of who she was as a woman and key character in the Bible.

Consider Ruth's trust in God and confidence in herself. She must have understood that, without any men remaining in Naomi's family, she would be solely responsible for her and Naomi's wellbeing. A daunting role was set before her if she chose to remain with Naomi. Yet, the author of Ruth's story depicts such a powerful conversation when Ruth commits to standing with Naomi without any hint of hesitation. Out of loss and heartbreak, we hear words of unity, unconditional love, and conviction.

Who or what motivates you to serve with determination? We are divinely called, and we answer this call with the strength and confidence of Almighty God supporting us. God honors our faithfulness. We are doing His Kingdom work. There are no limits to the outcome if we step forward in obedience with trust and determination. Ruth had no idea her commitment would lead to the Son of God being born in our world many years later. Who knows the impact your actions will have?

Today's Intention:

_____

_____

_____

_____

May the Lord Bless You and Keep You:

In the midst of heartbreak and heaviness, may you find the courage to rise up once again with determination.

When you experience joy and accomplishment, may you be richly blessed.

May the Holy Spirit fill you with unwavering trust in God and confidence in your purpose.

You are called to do this work for His purpose and glory.

You may not see the outcome right now, but your story is impacting countless others.

May you step forward in hope today.

Memorable Moment:

_____

_____

_____

_____

I AM CHANGING

"I hope I never give up on the reality that every person has the capacity to change."
~ Desmond Tutu & Mpho Tutu [70]

A potter, with their purposeful hands, reaches for a lump of clay. The clay feels ready, malleable, and full of potential. Knowing just the right maneuvers, the artist begins to knead the clay, shifting its position in various directions. The clay must be patient, as there will be many changes in its journey of becoming what the potter has envisioned. Many tools are used to mold and shape the composition. Some feel sharp, surprising, and bold. Others, like the potter's hands, feel familiar and comforting. On the potter's wheel, change becomes rhythmic as the swirling motion continues while the clay shifts in shape. When it comes time to be placed in the kiln, the once lump of dirt endures refining heat, enabling it to withstand the elements of the future. Finally, the craftsman adds their final touches, sharing their image and creativity with this purposeful vessel.

As the school year progresses, we may notice ourselves changing. We are on a journey of becoming our truest selves, moving and molding into who God has designed us to be. Like the clay, our hearts and minds must be pliable for deep change to take place. Similarly, our students are changing. Perhaps God has been shaping us, as educators, into potters as well, cultivating spaces where growing, changing, and risk-taking are welcome and safe. What tools and strategies can we bring to the classroom to help students shape their own unique design?

Conversely, we may not be seeing as much positive change as we thought we would at this point in the school year. This can feel discouraging. Here, we reflect on the hope of Desmond and Mpho Tutu: Everyone will have opportunities to change and grow. Remember, we are not alone. We are only one stage in the process for our students. Year by year, God will bring teachers and mentors who will continue to encourage students, adding layers of belief and belonging. This is one thing we know to be true: *God will never give up on the reality that every person has the capacity to change.*

Today's Intention:

_____

_____

_____

_____

May the Lord Bless You and Keep You:

May God develop and cultivate your life into the vessel He envisions.
May your heart be open to change and growth.
May you be inspired to chase after a healthy and authentic way of
living and loving.
May you notice subtle changes of others around you as evidence of
God's work.
And may the Holy Spirit strengthen your heart to hold onto the hope
that all people have the capacity to change.

Memorable Moment:

_____

_____

_____

_____

I AM TRANSFORMED

"Do not conform to the pattern of this world, but be transformed by the renewing of your mind. Then you will be able to test and approve what God's will is—his good, pleasing and perfect will."
~ Romans 12:2 (NIV)

Transformation is intentional, thoughtful, and sometimes unexpected. The action of transforming is grounded in God's purpose and calling for our lives. We are invited to be self-disciplined, focused, and ever in tune with Jesus. I have to admit, the word, "transform," scares me a bit. Transformation is a process that brings about a change of condition, which is almost always accompanied by a level of discomfort. However, we know there is no growth without discomfort.

When we make the decision to keep growing closer to God, loving others better, and embracing peace in the moment, we are courageously stepping into vulnerability. Our mindsets may be shifted and renewed. We may need to prayerfully break the cycle of unhealthy habits in order to be a vessel God can use for His glorious purpose. We invite space for freedom in our lives as we experience God's good, pleasing, and perfect will.

At this point in the year, I can imagine we have noticed transformation in our students and ourselves.

Where have you noticed evidence of change in yourself?

Are you proud of this change or does it feel discouraging?

How have your students transformed over the course of the school year?

What breakthroughs can you celebrate today?

Where are you continuing to trust God for His transformative work?

Today's Intention:

_____

_____

_____

_____

May the Lord Bless You and Keep You:

May this be a season of transformation.
May you see evidence of growth in your own heart and mind.
May God stir in you an awareness of how others are changing.
If you are waiting for a breakthrough, may you pray relentlessly, trusting that
God is orchestrating all things to fit together in His perfect timing.
And may you walk forward, confident that God is at work today.

Memorable Moment:

_____

_____

_____

_____

Part 6
I Am Celebrated

I AM CELEBRATED

"And so we celebrated because the Lord had indeed worked miracles for us. We cried on the way to plant our seeds, but we will celebrate and shout as we bring in the crops."
~ Psalm 126: 3, 6 (CEV)

We end our journey together in celebration. If we don't feel in a celebratory mood right now, that's okay. We will take thirty days to create space and time to reflect on and process this theme. Through the challenges, breakthroughs, regrets, and determination, we are celebrated.

God, the Author of your calling, celebrates *you*. Take a deep breath and allow that to sink in.

Every time you take a moment to help another person feel seen, known, and valued, you are celebrated. This displays empathy.

When you choose to step away from the classroom to show love to yourself or your loved ones, you are celebrated. This requires courage.

On the days you try something new or take risks because you know it is best for your students, you are celebrated. This demonstrates vulnerability.

And when you cry yourself to sleep or hit the punching bag a little harder, you are celebrated because, in these bitter moments, you allow yourself to *feel* and be *you*.

You have a Heavenly representation rooting for you, celebrating with you and for you. Even on the most disheartening days, Jesus empathizes with your journey. He is not looking at you in judgment or criticism. Rather, He celebrates the areas in which your heart is yearning to grow and the ways you continue to show love in all you do.

Today's Intention:

_____

_____

_____

_____

May the Lord Bless You and Keep You:
*May you celebrate in advance for the outcomes yet to be seen.
As you travel on this journey, may your mind be opened to how much
you are celebrated.
You are one of a kind, created intentionally and uniquely.
Today, may you take a quiet moment to reflect on the miracles God
has worked in and through you.*

Memorable Moment:

_____

_____

_____

_____

I AM JOYFUL

"For the Lord your God is living among you. He is a mighty savior. He will take delight in you with gladness. With his love, he will calm all your fears. He will rejoice over you with joyful songs."
~ Zephaniah 3:17 (NLT)

Today is a new day, filled with blessings God has prepared in advance for us! When we woke up this morning, the slate was wiped clean by the mercies of our gracious Heavenly Father. We have been called to make a difference in this world, to enlighten, encourage, and empower those around us. Rejoice and be glad in the abundant love of Jesus!

We are promised profound joy, even when we may not feel particularly happy. Joy is not contingent upon our current mood or shifting feelings. Rather, joyfulness is a deep awareness of our unbreakable connection with Jesus Christ. In our reflection verse, we read: *He will take delight in you with gladness. With his love, he will calm all your fears.* We are understood intimately. What a comforting truth! Jesus knows that, even when He is delighting over us with gladness, we may still feel anxious or unworthy. Therefore, in the midst of imperfection and busyness, we are invited to meditate on the truths we read in Scripture and rejoice in the promises of God!

The Lord your God is living among you in the classroom, office, playground, cafeteria, and library. No matter what our circumstances are, we can remain content and thankful because we are supported, comforted, and loved unconditionally. As we intentionally direct our thoughts toward God's faithfulness and grace, our joy increases because we are brought closer to the character of God, which is Joy itself!

Today's Intention:

_____

_____

_____

_____

May the Lord Bless You and Keep You:

May the Holy Spirit open your eyes to the blessings God has given you.
May your delight in these blessings bring forth joy, continually emanating in
and through you.
In moments when your heart may not feel overjoyed, may the Holy Spirit
bring a deep awareness of the peace and love of Christ.
May you feel the Lord your God living within you, rejoicing over you.
And may all your fears be calmed in the presence of His love.

Memorable Moment:

_____

_____

_____

_____

I AM ABUNDANT

**"The thief comes only to steal and kill and destroy.
I came that they may have life and have it abundantly."
~ John 10:10 (ESV)**

Steal, kill, and destroy. Those are words representative of an attack. Have you felt under attack at certain times this year? This looks so unique to each of us. Perhaps you find that creativity, passion, and empathy are slowly being stolen from your heart. You may be going through loss and heartbreak that is too painful to articulate with words. Or it may even feel as if life itself is crumbling around you. My friend, I am sorry you have gone through, or are going through, these times.

Jesus breaks it down abruptly. Without any sugar-coating, He identifies exactly what Satan intends to accomplish. He sees into our stolen, destroyed experiences and yet, in the very next breath, He comforts us with a promise. *I came that they may have life and have it abundantly.*

Did you know God's design for your life is abundance? God created you to be healthy and whole. Jesus is victorious! He is more powerful than Satan's schemes. Therefore, if His purpose is to give us an overflowing life, no other forces can hinder this. We can follow in obedience, trusting His timing, growth, and promises. We journey forward, choosing to have faith in God's provision and abundance in our daily experiences.

Today's Intention:

_____

_____

_____

_____

May the Lord Bless You and Keep You:
You are promised an abundant life.
Today, may you reflect on the challenges you and God have tackled together.
May the Holy Spirit protect against any schemes intended to rob you of abundant life.
May you look around you to see the blessings given in this moment.
And may you look forward in hope, trusting Christ's vision for your daily living.

Memorable Moment:

_____

_____

_____

_____

I AM LIFE

**"They were pleasant spring days, in which the winter of man's discontent was thawing as well as the earth, and the life that had lain torpid began to stretch itself."
~ Henry David Thoreau** [71]

I am life, blessed with life.
In this season, we stretch ourselves from torpidity to vigor.
From losing the motion and power of feeling,
To the breath of Fresh Air that only Spring can bring.
We are reminded, once again, of the essence of Life itself.

Remember to be patient,
For Christ has been patient with you.

Remember to listen,
For you know the feeling of being ignored.

Remember to empathize,
For everyone has their own story.

Remember to be kind,
For the world is full of hate.

Remember to fight with confidence and love,
For many need protection and advocacy.

Remember to be humble,
For one does not progress far when consumed with pride.

Remember to apologize,
For no one is perfect.

Remember to forgive,
For no one needs to carry the burden of bitterness.

Remember to love unconditionally,
For Christ has loved you all along life's journey.

Remember to have joy,
For God has blessed you abundantly.

This is Life.

Today's Intention:

_____

_____

_____

_____

May the Lord Bless You and Keep You:
Today, may you feel fully alive!
May you inhale breaths of Fresh Air that is the Holy Spirit.
May Jesus bring new life to your soul as the Spring invites new growth in the soil.
May the God of Life center you in purpose and meaning.
And may you remember to share compassion and love in all you do.

Memorable Moment:

_____

_____

_____

_____

I AM IMPACTFUL

"I think the teaching profession contributes more to the future of our society than any other single profession."
~ John Wooden [72]

Did you know Oprah Winfrey's spark for learning and creativity was inspired by her fourth-grade teacher? Perhaps you've heard the famous musical playwright, Lin Manuel-Miranda, was greatly influenced by a song his elementary music teacher wrote, the lyrics of which he can still recite today. John Legend has shared that his English teacher instilled confidence within him as a writer which led him on his path to songwriting. Dr. Maya Angelou was empowered by her neighbor, who was a teacher, to use her voice to create positive change.

These are bold examples of public figures who have been impacted by a teacher's love, words, and actions. However, what about the experiences not found on headlines or shared by celebrities? Consider the lives saved, hope instilled, and dreams cultivated, all because of an educator. Perhaps with an invitation, these stories will emerge as well. It is a powerful practice to ask those around you, "When you think about your teachers, who comes to mind?" "Who is the teacher who has had the most impact on your life?" You may be surprised by what you hear.

My high school Algebra teacher inspired me to be an educator when she watched me teach Vacation Bible School at my church when I was in eighth grade. Even before she knew I would be a student in her class that year, she introduced herself and asked me if I had ever considered being a teacher. She told me I had strength in this area. This belief, coupled with witnessing her unbelievable patience and empathy toward her students, influenced my decision to be an educator, and thus, impacted my life forever.

Today's Intention:

_____

_____

_____

_____

May the Lord Bless You and Keep You:

Today, you are impacting those around you.
May the Holy Spirit use your words and actions for purposes beyond your wildest imagination!
May you be encouraged by stories of the legacies teachers have left behind.
May you reflect on your own teachers who have positively impacted you.
And may you be empowered as you embrace, love, and value your students.

Memorable Moment:

_____

_____

_____

_____

I AM A STEWARD

"...that by such stewardship I might bring a greater order to my own life, and to the lives of any I'm given to serve, so that in those ordered spaces bright things might flourish: fellowship and companionship, creativity and conversation, learning and laughter, and enjoyment and health."
~ Douglas McKelvey [73]

We have been given a calling of great responsibility. God has placed lives in our care for a meaningful purpose. In our *ordered spaces* - our Holy classrooms - bright things have flourished this year. There have been difficult, dark days, but by God's grace and strength, we have arrived at today.

I wonder how fellowship and companionship have been cultivated in your classrooms and offices. How I would love to sit with you and hear your stories of surprising friendships, lessons learned, and teamwork! It would be a joy to witness the creativity and conversation inspired by your words and actions. I smile as I imagine the best learning and laughter moments from your year, memories that will remain with you well into the future. I hope there has been enjoyment and health in body and soul. You have been a nourisher, comforter, and advocate. God honors this loving spirit within you.

In all these responsibilities, you have been a faithful steward. With the Holy Spirit's leading, you have made difficult decisions, prioritized students, and journeyed forward on joyful and challenging days. You have impacted the lives you have been given to serve in unimaginable ways. God is using your stewardship for great purposes.

Today's Intention:

_____

_____

_____

_____

May the Lord Bless You and Keep You:

Today, may you view your life through a clearer lens because God has blessed you with this calling.

May the Holy Spirit fill you with confidence in knowing that you have made a difference this year.

May you be reminded of the joyful moments of learning and laughter.

May God bring to mind beautiful memories that may have faded through the days and weeks.

And may you feel proud of your stewardship, grounded in the purposes God has set before you.

Memorable Moment:

_____

_____

_____

_____

I AM STEADFAST

"Consistency of effort over the long run is everything."
~ Angela Duckworth [74]

It was the last day of school, and my students and I were saying our goodbyes outside as their parents gradually picked them up from school. One of the last to leave was a student I had for two years. When it was time to get on the bus, he was hesitant to say goodbye, but I told him how much I would miss him. He turned around to walk toward the bus, and I shouted, "Wait! Did you forget?" He turned around, his face puzzled then expectant as I showed him my closed fist to make a fist bump. He rushed back, gave me a fist bump, and my hand opened to reveal a small mint. The look on his face was indescribable. You see, for months this student had asked me for a mint at the end of every day. During our busy dismissal time, I would always try to remember to keep a mint ready, so when he and I fist bumped and said our goodbyes, one would be revealed. On this last day, he was surprised I had remembered to bring one out with us. I will never forget the look on his face and the trust that tiny mint cultivated.

This story is such a simple example, but I share it because I believe it illustrates that, as teachers, *consistency over the long run is everything*. We have demonstrated steadfastness in so many ways, responding with love on good and bad days alike. We have shown unwavering advocacy for our students when they are struggling or hurting, never giving up even though there were times when we entertained the thought. If the seemingly small action of remembering to give a mint at the end of the day could cultivate trust with a student, just imagine the impact of our steadfast efforts all year long.

Ultimately, we know this was not of our own doing. God has been and will be our constant support over the long run. The Holy Spirit has empowered us with strength on days when we did not know if we could continue. Jesus has walked with us in times when we were hurting and lonely. God's faithfulness has been present all along our journey this year, and will continue to be constant in whatever lies ahead.

Today's Intention:

_____

_____

_____

_____

May the Lord Bless You and Keep You:
You have shown great endurance and a steadfast spirit.
May you be given peace and honor when you think of the consistent efforts
you have taken.
May you continue to show unconditional love to those around you.
May the Holy Spirit instill in you gritty faith to run the race set before you.
And may God bless the work you have done and continue to do.

Memorable Moment:

_____

_____

_____

_____

I AM OBEDIENT

"And this is love: that we walk in obedience to his commands. As you have heard from the beginning, his command is that you walk in love."
~ 2 John 1:6 (NIV)

I have been called to give my all,
For Christ has given His all.
I have accepted the invitation and walked in obedient trust,
Empowered by the Holy Spirit to be the hands and feet of Christ.

I am His hands to gently place on Band-aids,
To give high fives and fist bumps,
To write notes of empathy,
To provide a tissue,
To supply snacks,
To clap in celebration as my students share their passions.
What busy, powerful, impactful hands they are!

I am His feet to walk beside in comfort.
To wait patiently,
To dance,
To bend down,
To stretch new muscles,
To walk the halls in love, obedient to His commands.
What an honor. What a calling!

Today's Intention:

_____

_____

_____

_____

May the Lord Bless You and Keep You:
Today, may you feel God's face shine upon you, bringing you peace.
May you be given glimpses of how your obedience has produced positive impacts in your community.
May your hard work, determination, and passion be honored, giving glory to God.
As you look to the remaining days of the school year, may you journey forward, taking each step in love.

Memorable Moment:

_____

_____

_____

_____

I AM A MENTOR

"Remember those who led you, who spoke the word of God to you; and considering the result of their way of life, imitate their faith."
~ Hebrews 13:7 (NASB)

Not long into my teaching career, I began a practice that I still continue. Its purpose is to identify teachers and leaders I look up to and the reasons why I hold them in high regard. This list of people and their attributes provides inspiration for areas in my life I want to develop. When you have a few moments, I invite you to join me by identifying these individuals in your own life. You could write down your reflections or simply allow your mind to engage in this exercise.

Think of a teacher you've had at some point in your life whom you admire. What do you appreciate about them? How did they interact with students? What words would you use to describe them?

Now think about a colleague, past or present, whom you respect greatly. What inspires you about this person? How do they make you feel? What practices do they employ that are the most impactful with students or coworkers?

Hopefully, thinking about these inspirational mentors leaves you feeling safe, valued, and inspired. Now consider how you want your students to feel today. What actions can you put into practice to help your students feel included and worthy of belonging? Will you be the teacher a student remembers as a leader who instilled encouragement and hope?

(I don't normally suggest intentions, however, today would be a great day to text, email, or call a teacher who inspires you. Thank them. Be specific about what they do that inspires your teaching. We need more of this in our world.)

Today's Intention:

_____

_____

_____

_____

May the Lord Bless You and Keep You:

Today, may your thoughts be filled with empowering leaders.
May you remember those who encouraged you, uplifted you, and believed in you.
By their example, may you be inspired to be intentional with your words and actions.
May you give a genuine compliment, thank someone dear to you, and genuinely listen.
And may your loving legacy remain with all who know you.

Memorable Moment:

_____

_____

_____

_____

I AM ILLUSTRATIVE

"Children learn more from what you are than what you teach."
~ W.E.B. DuBois [75]

One of my favorite parts about the end of the school year is the comradery I feel with my students. They know me and I know them. We recognize each other's quirks, struggles, and triumphs. We are learning in a community built on the values and boundaries we've created. Our team is not like the class next door, the class the year before, nor the class next year. We have developed a truly special atmosphere.

If given enough time, almost all students will get to know who and what teachers are, for better or for worse! So it is important that we, as educators, know who and what we are. We should be grounded in our identity and values, so we are modeling healthy, uplifting, and inspiring practices. Illustrative means to show something clearly. We are most impactful when we can demonstrate clearly that all students have value in our space, everyone has potential for growth, and all people are deserving of dignity. When we spend time in reflection, identifying our values, we will become more intentional about displaying evidence of those values in our lives.

This year, we have shown in subtle, consistent ways who we are and Whose we are. We began our journey together, centered on our calling from God, knowing we are named, claimed, equipped, and empowered. Nothing has the ability to overcome those truths. Because God has first loved us, we walk forward demonstrating our unconditional love toward those around us.

Today's Intention:

_____

_____

_____

_____

May the Lord Bless You and Keep You:

Today, may you be illustrative, demonstrating what you are, who you are, and Whose you are.
May you clearly show your identity and love in your spaces of learning.
May the Holy Spirit use your faithful obedience to instill messages of hope and worthiness into your students.
And by your example, may your students have a sense of belonging, embracing who they are as God has designed them, and illustrating strong, positive values in the world.

Memorable Moment:

_____

_____

_____

_____

I AM WEATHERED

**"You're blessed when you're at the end of your rope.
With less of you there is more of God and his rule."
~ Matthew 5:3 (MSG)**

One definition of "weathered" is to be seasoned by exposure to the elements. This year, we have been exposed to many uplifting and challenging experiences. Some may have impacted us in a way that will last for many years, shifting our thoughts or actions. Whether we realize it or not, God is building strength in us during the difficult times. Seasoned means to be effective by experience. We have journeyed through storms, endured rain, snow, hail, scorching sun - all the elements - and have been changed because of it.

You're blessed when you're at the end of your rope.

We reflect with tired and grateful hearts, acknowledging that throughout the seasons, God has been strengthening us by exposure to the elements. We are stronger educators now than we were six months ago. Out of hardships, resilience and wisdom have emerged, thus seasoning us for the future. Without having been exposed to the elements, our impact would be less effective.

With less of you there is more of God and his rule.

When we surrender our reflexive need for comfort and ease, distanced from the storms, we find ourselves in places of risk and mystery. It may feel like there is *less of us* because we open our hands and hearts to loosen control. However, when we do this, we invite room for the Holy Spirit to use our lives for glorious purposes. Whether you are in a time of celebration or fatigue, God is actively working through your experiences, seasoning you for the journey ahead.

Today's Intention:

_____

_____

_____

_____

May the Lord Bless You and Keep You:
*On days when you feel at the end of your rope, may you be blessed.
May the Holy Spirit reveal how you have been seasoned by
your experiences.
May you receive the freedom to open your hands and heart, inviting
God to lead your steps.
May you rest in God's timing and purposes, knowing they are
perfectly planned.*

Memorable Moment:

_____

_____

_____

_____

I AM PERSEVERANT

"Not only so, but we also glory in our sufferings, because we know that suffering produces perseverance; perseverance, character; and character, hope. And hope does not put us to shame, because God's love has been poured out into our hearts through the Holy Spirit, who has been given to us."
~ Romans 5:3-5 (NIV)

Because God's love has been poured out into our hearts through the Holy Spirit

This is where we began our journey so many months ago, dwelling on the truths of our identity. We are called, claimed, and loved. Because God's love has filled our lives, through the power of the Holy Spirit, we have been inspired and uplifted to teach, learn, and love those around us. We begin and end in the love of God. Amen and Amen!

Suffering produces perseverance

Perseverance means continuing to work toward something despite challenges, failure, or opposition. Suffering and difficulties are required in order to develop perseverance. Even though it might sound cliché, we truly cannot develop strength and determination unless we endure hardships, drawing on God's unfailing faithfulness to inspire growth within us.

Perseverance, character, and character, hope

Through our suffering and perseverance, character is born. Character consists of our moral excellence - how we treat others and ourselves. When we have endured suffering, we are better equipped to empathize with the experiences of others, deepening the connection of our humanity. We become a community of people who have known times of pain, but who refuse to let those challenges hinder us from our purpose. As God has designed, we grow closer together, strengthening our hope.

And hope does not put us to shame.

Today's Intention:

_____

_____

_____

_____

May the Lord Bless You and Keep You:
Today, may you be strengthened in mind, body, and soul.
May Jesus be your Hope to press onward when challenges arise.
May your experiences lead you to connect with and empower others.
Through your suffering, perseverance, character, and hope, may
God be glorified!

Memorable Moment:

_____

_____

_____

_____

I AM WORN

"Share each other's burdens, and in this way obey the law of Christ."
~ Galatians 6:2 (NLT)

God, when I am worn,
Reveal to me who You are.
Demonstrate Your powerful love in miraculous ways.
Show Your strength when I am weak.
Impart Your peace that passes all understanding
In every space of learning today.
Remind me of Your faithfulness.

Jesus, when I am worn,
Walk with me through my day.
Thank You for never leaving me on my own.
Help me develop the determination You had in Your calling.
Open my eyes to see those who may need support or comfort.
As You have listened to me, help me listen to others well.
As you have loved me, help me to love others unconditionally.

Holy Spirit, when I am worn,
Lead others to come alongside me in gracious support.
Help me accept the words or actions my soul needs to embrace.
Open my eyes to see those You have already positioned in my midst.
As You have shared my burdens,
Unify Your people to share one another's burdens,
In this way, obeying the law of Christ.

Today's Intention:

_____

_____

_____

_____

May the Lord Bless You and Keep You:
On the days you feel worn, may you feel the Holy Spirit's wide expanse of grace, reaching out to bring you peace.
May your mind shift to what is truly important in these days.
Amid the ongoing demands, may you prioritize those who God has placed around you.
They are truly the most important.

Memorable Moment:

_____

_____

_____

_____

I AM SUPPORTED

"In his kindness God called you to share in his eternal glory by means of Christ Jesus. So after you have suffered for a little while, he will restore, support, and strengthen you, and he will place you on a firm foundation."
~ 1 Peter 5:10 (NLT)

Today is a good day to reflect on the people God has placed in your life to support you this year. You may want to write down your thoughts as you ask and answer questions, identifying the significant people around you and the faithfulness of God, our Rock.

Who are the people who have consistently supported you and shown up for you?
Were there any new or surprising supporters this year?
Have there been days when your students lifted you up when you needed it most?
In what ways have your colleagues helped shape you into a stronger person and teacher?

Ultimately, God is your biggest supporter. He has restored, empowered, and strengthened you, placing you on a firm foundation. There has never been a day, nor will there ever be, when God has not been with you, rooting for you even in the most difficult seasons.

When were moments this year you experienced the Holy Spirit moving in your learning space?
Were there days you felt God's grace in a deeper way?
What are some verses and quotes that have supported you on your journey?

Today's Intention:

_____

_____

_____

_____

May the Lord Bless You and Keep You:
Today, may you feel richly blessed by your support system.
May you create intentional moments to express gratitude to those who have supported you.
May you spend time in prayer, thanking and praising God for His provision and grace in your life.
Grounded on your firm foundation in Christ, may your strength be used to support those around you.

Memorable Moment:

_____

_____

_____

_____

I AM RESTORED

**"Christ be with me, Christ within me.
Christ behind me, Christ before me.
Christ beside me, Christ to win me.
Christ to comfort and restore me."
~ Prayer of St. Patrick [76]**

Restoration means to repair or work on something to return it to its original condition. At one point in my life, I was in a place where I lost sight of who I was. I had experienced some challenges and wondered if I could ever go back to the person I was before. I pondered what the coming days and weeks would hold. I am thankful for how God has remained faithful and rekindled passions within me. I am now able to look in the mirror and recognize myself again.

However, if you are reading this today and find yourself in that difficult space, waiting and praying for restoration, know that you are not alone. We long for a time when life didn't feel so heavy, chaotic, or painful. Our Savior does restore; however, I wonder if He views restoration differently than we do. I am not convinced He wants us to return to our original condition. Rather, I believe He uses the trials we have experienced to mold and shape us into the person He is creating us to be.

We will have difficult seasons in our life, but we will also have times when we find our hopes and dreams again, when we feel unconditionally loved and surprisingly joyful. When we invite God to do His restoration work within us, we will come out of the challenges a little changed, a little stronger, and perhaps even a little more compassionate toward others.

Today's Intention:

_____

_____

_____

_____

May the Lord Bless You and Keep You:
Today, may you feel restored in your body, mind, and spirit.
May God lift you up and set your spirit on new ground.
May the Holy Spirit give you grace and hope in this season of waiting.
May you be reminded of your hopes, dreams, and passions.
And may you walk in Truth today, knowing Christ is with you every step of the way.

Memorable Moment:

_____

_____

_____

_____

I AM HEALED

"He heals the brokenhearted and binds up their wounds."
~ Psalm 147:3 (NIV)

Imagine sitting next to a calm, isolated stream of water. Jesus walks up to where you're sitting and kindly asks if He can join you. You invite Him to sit down. He can sense the weight you are carrying. The worries, fears, grief, pain, sacrifice, and exhaustion. It feels like He knows your every thought: the questions you are navigating, the conversations you are replaying, and the messages you are telling yourself. "Do you want to talk about it?" Jesus asks. You may take this opportunity to pour out your heart, saying all of the things that have been left unsaid for far too long. Or you may sit in silence, any words you express feeling too complicated or painful. After either response, Jesus listens and waits. Then He warmly takes hold of your hand and asks, "Do you want to be healed?"

Your answer will set you on the next steps of your journey. If you respond "Yes," you are inviting Jesus to enter with you into your thoughts, your places of hurt, and the experiences that perhaps you'd rather keep hidden. It may feel uncomfortable and vulnerable to go to these spaces or have them exposed, even just between the two of you. Because when your pain is identified, you are no longer free to dismiss it and push it down again. You must reach out for Jesus' hand to deal with this hurt together so it does not deal with you.

If you respond "Yes" to Jesus' healing power, you are saying "No" to Satan and his influence over your experiences. Your hurt is valid and has impacted who you are today, but to be truly healed, you must allow Jesus to lead you in forgiving yourself and others. Forgiveness defeats the hold shame and guilt have held over you. Emotional, spiritual, and physical healing require you to make decisions that move you in the direction of wholeness, as God designed for you.

Do you want to be healed?

Today's Intention:

_____

_____

_____

_____

May the Lord Bless You and Keep You:

Today, may you take hold of your Heavenly Healer's hand.
May you not feel defeated by confusion and unanswered questions.
May you be filled with the presence of Jesus in this moment.
When you experience breakthrough and healing, may you rejoice and be thankful!
In times of heartbreak and suffering, may you feel surrounded by love and empathy.

Memorable Moment:

_____

_____

_____

_____

I AM THANKFUL

"Some people could be given an entire field of roses and only see the thorns in it. Others could be given a single weed and only see the wildflower in it. Perception is a key component to gratitude. And gratitude a key component to joy."
~ Amy Weatherly [77]

Many emotional-health researchers have pointed to the importance of gratitude in our ongoing wellness. People who write down or verbalize who and what they are thankful for often have a more optimistic view of life and are able to be more present in the moment. Being grateful is certainly supported by Scripture. Many verses in the Old and New Testaments remind us that thankfulness is a direct result of our faith.

Yet, it is so easy to go about our days and miss opportunities to reflect on our blessings. As Amy Weatherly articulates, the way we perceive our experiences impacts our positive or negative view of those moments. We have all met people who, even in the midst of seemingly unbearable circumstances, are some of the most positive, thankful people we have ever met! There is something warm and inviting about being in the company of people who are authentically appreciative.

If we want to develop our gratitude and notice the *wildflowers in the weeds*, we have the freedom to begin! It starts with today. We can notice blessings around us and become more comfortable with telling others we are grateful for who they are and the gifts they share. At the beginning or end of the day, we can set aside a minute to write down five things for which we are thankful. This practice alone can turn our mindset in a more positive direction. When these practices feel new or uncomfortable, the Holy Spirit will bring contentment and ideas to mind if we are open to receiving them.

Today's Intention:

_____

_____

_____

_____

May the Lord Bless You and Keep You:
Today, may you be mindful and thankful.
May God bring to your attention the countless blessings He has placed in your life.
May you find moments to tell others how thankful you are for them.
May your gratitude be contagious, like a spark igniting a flame.
And may your perspective begin to reflect God's perspective in everything you do.

Memorable Moment:

_____

_____

_____

_____

I AM CONFLICTED

"Allow the Lord, by his love and grace, to let you live in this moment. Right now. This moment is as perfect as it can be. And God's call, the needs of the world, will make itself very apparent. Just respond to the need that presents itself right in front of you, today, tomorrow."
~ Richard Rohr [78]

We may find ourselves in the middle of conflicting feelings. Many of us are ready for this year to come to a close, wishing the best for our students as they move forward. However, we may also feel regret or concern. Perhaps we invested time, energy, and love into certain students, and we are not seeing the progress we had hoped for. We may be thinking about our learners who rely on us and the school structure for support, and are worried about what their futures will look like without this.

We have permission to sit with the "both - and" of these feelings. With so many shifting emotions, it may be difficult to be present in the moment, however, this is where the Holy Spirit speaks life into us. In Scripture, we read reminders that God rejoices over us and the impact we create. We also hear invitations to lay our burdens at the feet of Jesus, as He offers us the promise of abundant life.

In our complexities, uncertainties, and conflicting feelings, we have permission to give ourselves grace and time to sit with our wrestling souls. Jesus meets us here and promises to take each moment with us. Maybe today we will just be present, focusing on the students and colleagues around us. As we breathe in the Holy Spirit and exhale surrendering prayers and praises to God, we move forward with the freedom to enjoy the time we have with the ones God has blessed us with this year.

Today's Intention:

_____

_____

_____

_____

May the Lord Bless You and Keep You:

Today, may the Holy Spirit bless your mind and heart with peace.
May you give yourself grace for your conflicting feelings and ideas.
May God reveal the needs of the world through ways you can make
an impact.
And may you feel invited to be present in this moment,
simply journeying with Jesus.

Memorable Moment:

_____

_____

_____

_____

I AM CONTENT

**"You're blessed when you're content with just who you are -
no more, no less. That's the moment you find yourselves
proud owners of everything that can't be bought."
~ Matthew 5:5 (MSG)**

As we near the end of a long year, your mind may be racing with
all of the remaining tasks. You may have the continual nagging of
an unresolved problem, feel hurried by the many activities in
your schedule, or remember a phone call you were supposed to
make two months ago! In this time of excitement, energy, and
fluctuating emotions, it may be difficult to feel content.

Whether or not your goals have been met, it is okay. You are not
measured by the work you do, the conversations you have, or
the victories won. You are not defined by your students' end-of-
the-year assessment results. Your worth is not measured by the
academic or behavioral progress made. God honors your work
and its lasting impact; however, your value to God is not based
on your actions. You are named and claimed as a child of God.
Nothing will ever change this promise.

At the core of God's character is His love for you. Out of this love
comes a passion to see you grow into the person He has
envisioned: healthy, peace-filled, joyful, and impactful. Your
identity, worth, and purpose are in Christ - and Christ alone.
Only by His work on the cross are you made perfect and whole.
In wholeness, you find contentment. In Jesus, you are at peace
with exactly who you are and inspired to press onward in the
development of who you are becoming.

Today's Intention:

_____

_____

_____

_____

May the Lord Bless You and Keep You:
Today, may you be content.
May you reflect on what you are thankful for about your calling.
In the midst of striving and waiting, may you feel at peace in this moment.
When unsettledness enters your mind and heart, may you trust God with answers and outcomes.
May the Holy Spirit bless you as you develop contentment in who you are - no more, no less.
And may you be centered on Jesus, who is the Source of all healing and wholeness.

Memorable Moment:

_____

_____

_____

_____

I AM PROUD

"Pray and thank God for having chosen you to live this life and do this work."
~ Mother Teresa [79]

(My sister has been an incredible first-grade teacher for over 17 years. After a particularly difficult school day for her, I wrote her a letter. I would like to share this letter today as my message to you as well.)

Dear Teacher,

I'm so proud of you. On days when it feels so very heavy, I am proud of you for walking forward and loving harder. For the millions of decisions you make every day, always asking first, "What is best for our kids?" For the lunch breaks you sacrifice to clean up after a meltdown. For the phone calls, emails, texts, and pleads in the office. I'm proud of you for advocating for your students.

I'm proud of the impact you have made and will make. Hundreds of students' lives are brighter, more inspired, and more empathetic because you have been their teacher. You've never given up on them. You kindle kindness in those little hearts. You listen and love unconditionally. They know it - they can feel it.

What I am most proud of about you is that, on the best breakthrough days and on the hardest heartbreaking days, you always thank God you live this life and do this work. You take pride in what you do because you are so confident the Holy Spirit will create a positive impact through your words, actions, and love. You are the humblest person I've ever met, yet you display such incredible pride in our profession. I am encouraged by your example every day.

Thank you. I am proud of you - more than you know. You are loved and valued.

Love, Christina

Today's Intention:

_____

_____

_____

_____

May the Lord Bless You and Keep You:

Today, may you feel how proud God is of your love and devotion this year.
May you know without doubt that your labor has made a Kingdom impact.
In humility, may you be proud of yourself for the times you said "Yes" when
it would have been easier to say "No."
May you feel a fierce pride for your students, reflecting on their
growth and determination.
May you pray and thank God for having chosen you to live this life and do
this work.

Memorable Moment:

_____

_____

_____

_____

I AM PASSIONATE

"Effective teaching may be the hardest job there is."
~ William Glasser [80]

Real Talk Time. Teaching effectively is an incredibly challenging calling. On days when we feel low and lonely, hopelessness may surface in our hearts and minds. We may lose sight of our purpose and dreams. We may even feel as if our past is brighter than our future could ever be. I am comforted by the truth that, whether we are beginning, in the middle of, or ending our school year, the passions God has placed in our hearts are alive and well.

Our purpose is not conditional, based on our shifting feelings. Our passions are waiting for us to work them into fruition by God's grace and leading. We journey through celebratory moments and difficult days, each season necessary to walk through in order to truly embrace and cultivate our passions. The Holy Spirit uses our experiences as an invitation to shift our focus to our God-given goals and dreams, finding opportunities to nourish and develop them. We are only stuck if we choose not to move forward. We are only isolated if we choose not to reach out to others. We can only lose hope completely if we take our eyes off of Christ and His faithfulness in our lives.

Today, I invite you to take a few moments - maybe right now or maybe later in the day - to reflect on the hopes and dreams God has designed in your heart. They are alive within you. Perhaps they need to be remembered and seen to spark the passion to chase them again. Who knows what the future may hold!

Today's Intention:

_____

_____

_____

_____

May the Lord Bless You and Keep You:
May your hidden dreams and passions resurface in exciting ways.
May you be reminded of why you began this journey.
May the Holy Spirit show you parts of yourself that are
awaiting discovery!
And out of your passions, may new and wonderful paths be formed.

Memorable Moment:

_____

_____

_____

_____

I AM WISE

"For the Lord gives wisdom; from his mouth come knowledge and understanding."
~ Proverbs 2:6 (NIV)

A wise person is able to discern internal qualities and relationships, having a deep understanding about the world around them. When we seek to view the people we meet and the world we explore through God's perspective, wisdom is developed. We listen with openness and empathy. We observe with curiosity and compassion.

The Lord gives wisdom. We have been given the incredible gift of Scripture to support our knowledge and understanding. Teaching, leadership, and life itself are stronger, more effective, and more powerful when insight is sought through God's Word. We are reminded of God's unconditional love, direction, purpose, and compassion. As we read, we draw on the Holy Spirit to move and change us, bringing us closer to Jesus and His example.

The Holy Spirit is another beautiful gift which causes our hearts and minds to find freedom in openness and opportunity. Our Guide stirs in us questions and wonderings, inviting new perspectives and practices. In what ways have you grown in wisdom through your experiences this year? Let's consider these questions as we reflect on the past days, weeks, and months.

What lessons have your students taught you?

What have you learned from your colleagues and leaders?

What beliefs or perspectives have been shifted?

What new insights will you take with you as you journey forward?

How have you grown in your understanding of God?

What have you learned about yourself?

What questions are you still exploring?

Today's Intention:

_____

_____

_____

_____

May the Lord Bless You and Keep You:

Today, may you authentically reflect on all you have learned this year.
May the Holy Spirit give you wisdom and understanding in all you do.
Where there is mystery and unanswered questions, may your trust in Jesus deepen.
And may you use the wisdom you have gained to cultivate community around you.

Memorable Moment:

_____

_____

_____

_____

I AM CARING

"You're blessed when you care. At the moment of being 'care-full,' you find yourself being cared for."
~ Matthew 5:7 (MSG)

At the end of one school year, a student made a card for me. In this note, he wrote several sweet ideas, but one sentence stood out to me the most. It read: "You are the only teacher I've had to say good morning to me every day." As this student reflected on his fifth-grade year, the closure of his elementary school experience, this is what stood out to him. It made me pause. Greeting students every morning was natural for me, something that didn't require a second thought.

His note of recognition reminded me that perhaps we, as teachers, put more pressure on ourselves than is necessary. We often strive for the perfect lesson or organized lab stations. We may think to ourselves, *If I just plan a little bit more, prepare another activity, or develop a brand-new behavior system, tomorrow will be better.* And maybe our preparations will bring about positive results. However, we may overlook the seemingly simple actions that demonstrate how much we care. Our daily practices of listening to stories, making eye contact, smiling as every student enters our space, laughing about the silly things, and showing empathy when challenges arise are just a few examples. These moments may be the most impactful memories, lasting a lifetime.

Jesus brings us a powerful message. When we fill our days with authentic care toward others, *we find ourselves being cared for.* God is in the light we share, the kindness we extend, and the choices we make. The Holy Spirit enters these holy moments and blesses us and others with deep joy. Let us treat one another with care and stay alert to the amazing work God is doing in and through our lives!

Today's Intention:

_____

_____

_____

_____

May the Lord Bless You and Keep You:

Today, may you feel affirmed in your daily acts of love and care.
May the Holy Spirit guide your words and actions as you prioritize
caring for those around you.
May you be blessed as you represent Christ's light and love in your
space of learning.
And may you find yourself cared for in your personal and
professional journey.

Memorable Moment:

_____

_____

_____

_____

I AM A COMMUNICATOR

"Words are, in my not-so-humble opinion, our most inexhaustible source of magic. Capable of both inflicting injury, and remedying it."
~ J.K. Rowling [81]

The end of the school year invites an opportunity to communicate truths to your students. Whether you have twenty students or two hundred, consider how you might inspire them with your words. Pray over these messages and ideas. Ask the Holy Spirit to fill you with declarations that will provide lifelong encouragement to each student.

What characteristics, strengths, and skills have you noticed about each student?

What do you believe for the future of your students?

In their joyful and challenging seasons of life, what do you want to make sure your students remember?

During the last few weeks of school, I often write my students individual letters and, as a team, I share my most important life lessons. Usually, we focus on one each day, leading up to the last day of school. I tell my students, "If you only remember these lessons from our entire year together, that will be enough."

Life Lessons from Ms. Meline:
Lesson #1: You are always worthy of dignity and respect.
Lesson #2: Life is more simple than you think. Work hard and be kind.
Lesson #3: You are not alone.
Lesson #4: Be the change.

Your messages will be unique to you and your students. This is incredibly special. As the end of the year draws closer and our exhaustion sets in, let us push forward and continue to leave a legacy while we still have them in our midst.

Today's Intention:

_____

_____

_____

_____

May the Lord Bless You and Keep You:

Today, may you intentionally reflect on the power of words.
May the Holy Spirit speak through you, providing truths your students so
desperately need to hear.
May your words remain in the hearts and minds of these young people.
And may God use your energy and empathy to create a
world-changing impact.

Memorable Moment:

_____

_____

_____

_____

I AM UNFORGETTABLE

"I've learned that people will forget what you said, people will forget what you did, but people will never forget how you made them feel."
~ Maya Angelou [82]

I will never forget the feeling,
Stepping into Miss' room every day.
It felt like stepping into myself.
There was a warmth and beauty about the space
That didn't come from old cupboards and worn textbooks.
I know where it came from - straight from her heart.
She had a way of listening, of knowing us inside and out.
She could glance at us in the hallway
And instantly know something was wrong.
Miss always had the right words to say - like magic.
It was unexplainable - unforgettable.

What I remember about Mister is his smile.
It would light up the whole room!
It wouldn't matter if you just failed a test or got bullied during recess.
In Mister's room, you were important just for being you.
But it was more than that.
Mister believed in us - truly believed.
His eyes got wide and intent every time we shared an answer or story.
You would've thought he was hearing a world-famous speech!
Nothing could compete for his attention when he was around us.
It was unbelievable - unforgettable.

Today's Intention:

_____

_____

_____

_____

May the Lord Bless You and Keep You:

May you honor and cherish each student God has given you to love.
May the Holy Spirit empower your words and actions.
May those around you feel seen, known, and valued by you.
May you be unforgettable, leaving a lasting legacy of hope and love.

Memorable Moment:

_____

_____

_____

_____

I AM PEACE-FILLED

"These things I have spoken to you, that in me you may have peace. In the world you will have tribulation; but be of good cheer, I have overcome the world."
~ John 16:33 (NKJV)

We have traveled through many days together. Perhaps you find yourself reflecting on all you have encountered: challenges you didn't anticipate, unexpected health concerns, or new and exciting transformations. Maybe you are looking back on everything you have overcome by the grace of God. Memories may be rushing back reminding you of breakthrough moments and subtle celebrations. You may be thinking of prayers answered, and perhaps some still waiting for God's timing.

In our reflection times, we have meditated on God's promises to us. The words of authors, teachers, and speakers have inspired our minds to think creatively and purposefully. Questions have been asked and answered as we have navigated this journey we call teaching. We return to messages of hope and peace because this belief is what enables us to be filled with peace in our daily interactions and responsibilities. We can breathe deeply and rest in the reality that Jesus knows the bigger picture, and He holds the past, present, and future in His loving hands.

Jesus said, *Consider these things I have spoken to you, that in me you may have peace.*

I am the way, the truth, and the life. (John 14:6)
Peace be with you. As the Father has sent me, even so I am sending you. (John 20:21)
Peace I leave with you; my peace I give to you. Not as the world gives do I give to you. Let not your hearts be troubled, neither let them be afraid. (John 14:27)

Today's Intention:

_____

_____

_____

_____

May the Lord Bless You and Keep You:

Today, may you inhale deep Holy Spirit breaths as you move through your day.

When anxieties and questions rise to the surface of your mind, may you turn your gaze back to the face of Jesus.

May you listen closely to His voice as He reminds you of His peace that passes all understanding.

Out of this peace, may you cherish these sweet moments with your students.

Memorable Moment:

_____

_____

_____

_____

I AM BITTERSWEET

**"Time slips. Days pass. Years fade. And life ends.
And what we came to do must be done while there is time."
~ Max Lucado [83]**

It was the morning before the last day of school. I had twenty more minutes of prep time before the bell rang and thirty energetic fifth-graders would be entering our classroom. As I checked off tasks on my to-do list, there was a knock at the door. A teacher was standing with one of my students. He had clearly been crying. "Can he hang out here until school starts?" she asked. "Of course!" I responded. "Let's sit down for a minute."

To this day, this student remains one the most resilient people I have ever met. He had experienced more hurt and pain in his life up to this point than most people encounter in a lifetime. Through it all, he remained hopeful and empathetic. He was the student who made me question my professional choice, but also inspired me to get out of bed in the morning. And at the end of the year, this sweetheart was quietly sobbing, head on his desk, because the school year was ending, and he was losing a significant source of security.

The end of the year feels bittersweet. We are ready for a much-deserved break, but we are not ready to let go. So often we want to fix all the problems – all the brokenness, pain, and traumatic memories. In that moment with my hurting student, I could not fix it. I could not take his worries or sadness away. But I could sit with him, empathize, and give him a hug. We are reminded that we are not their savior and we cannot pretend to be. Jesus is - and will be - with our students in whatever they face today and for the rest of their lives. We can take a deep breath, enjoy the beautiful moments, and trust God with the future.

Today's Intention:

_____

_____

_____

_____

May the Lord Bless You and Keep You:
Today, may you be present in the moments you share with those around you.
May you find sweetness in the midst of the bitter.
May your faith be strengthened as you trust God with the future.
And may you treasure each moment of your calling.

Memorable Moment:

_____

_____

_____

_____

I AM FAITHFUL

"His master replied, 'Well done, good and faithful servant! You have been faithful with a few things; I will put you in charge of many things. Come and share your master's happiness.'"
~ Matthew 25:23 (NIV)

When I was growing up, I became friends with a wonderful woman named Ethel. Ethel was in her seventies when we started going out for lunches and treats. She became another grandparent to me. When I was in middle school and moved to another town, we wrote letters back and forth to each other. She would always include a verse and tell me she was praying for me. My faithful Ethel.

Through high school and college, I would visit Ethel as often as I could. She was thrilled I had decided to be a teacher because that was her profession as well. She would excitedly provide nuggets of wisdom like, "I never had any behavior issues in the classroom. But you know, I'd go out and play with them during recess, so I think that's why. They knew when it was time to play and when it was time to work."

When Ethel turned ninety, I gave her a blank journal. I asked her to write in it for me and return it whenever it was filled. My faithful friend did just that. A few years later, a worn and loved journal came back to me. I didn't read a word of it, but instead, carefully placed it on my bookshelf for the right time.

We continued to write letters back and forth, but eventually, fewer and fewer arrived from her. The day Ethel passed away, at the age of ninety-nine, I went to my bookshelf and held her journal. I felt her warmth, opened it, and began to read her words. To this day, I have not finished reading her collection of wisdom and love. I know I will still need her letters, her words of faith, and her comfort. Ethel was a faithful teacher, friend, and disciple. She is now *sharing in her Master's happiness.*

Today's Intention:

_____

_____

_____

_____

May the Lord Bless You and Keep You:
Well done, good and faithful servant!
May God richly bless you for your faithfulness in the tasks He has set
before you.
May you trust that your obedient actions will leave a legacy, inspiring
future generations.
By your loyalty, love, and faith, may God's Kingdom
be strengthened.
May you reflect in gratitude and share in God's happiness today.

Memorable Moment:

_____

_____

_____

_____

I AM REFLECTIVE

"How lucky I am to have something that makes saying goodbye so hard."
~ A.A. Milne [84]

Pause.

All it takes is a moment to pause

To realize how beautiful the "little things" truly are.

Life is full of hard decisions and heartbreaking goodbyes,

Some expected and some not.

One does not know another's journey,

But in one moment, the journey may be shifted.

So smile at a stranger.

Give hugs.

Tell others they are important.

Reflect on meaningful memories,

And let them inspire forward movement.

Remember, days are made to be lived to the fullest.

And life is made up of moments in which we pause.

Today's Intention:

_____

_____

_____

_____

May the Lord Bless You and Keep You:
Today, may you be given grace to pause.
May you reflect with gratitude on all you have been given.
May you take advantage of every opportunity to build up those around you.
May memories stir in your heart, blessing you beyond anticipation.
And may you live today to the fullest.

Memorable Moment:

_____

_____

_____

_____

I AM FAVORED

"The Lord bless you, and keep you; The Lord make His face shine on you, and be gracious to you; The Lord lift up His countenance on you, and give you peace."
~ Numbers 6:24-26 (NASB)

My Friend,

Teacher, advocate, and child of God. Thank you for journeying with me through this school year. Thank you for caring so deeply about our young people. How I wish I could be sitting next to you today as you process the end of this year, balancing excitement, sadness, joy, and weariness. How I would love to hear your stories and learn from your lessons. What amazing testimonies of God's faithfulness we could share!

In a special way, I have felt as though I have been with you during our reflections, the Holy Spirit connecting us by God's design. We are not alone on this voyage. We are surrounded by others who are called to the classroom, empowered by the matchless energy of Christ to create an impact in our world. As we look closely, we will find more disciples who are courageous and compassionate as they run the race. In celebration, we will join them, encouraging and nourishing one another as we take one step in front of the other.

Our Heavenly Teacher is cultivating a community where all voices are welcome and uplifted, where we feel inspired to push ourselves to new heights for His glory, all the while living graciously toward ourselves and others. He holds out His hand and invites us to step into the next adventure with Him. I pray our paths will cross in this life or the next. You are an extraordinary human being! May God bless you richly.

With love, Christina

Today's Intention:

_____

_____

_____

_____

May the Lord Bless You and Keep You:

Today, may you feel blessed beyond measure as you entrust your students into God's care.
May you feel the warmth of God's radiant face shining on you.
As Jesus lifts up His countenance upon you, may you rest, gazing in His loving eyes.
And may the Holy Spirit fill you with grace and peace for the next steps in your journey.

Memorable Moment:

_____

_____

_____

_____

GOING DEEPER
Intention Examples

Setting intentions became a consistent daily practice early on in my professional career. I found it very powerful and effective to identify a focus for the day. For me, intentions can be personal or professional, specific or broad, eloquent or messy, practical or whimsical. You may even pray for the Holy Spirit to bring an intention to your mind. The purpose is to make the intentions meaningful to you and your calling that day. The following are examples of intentions I have taken out of my journals:

- Look for ways to build up those around me. What can I do or say to convey that each person has value and I am happy to see them? What can I do to bring out the positive gifts and strengths of my kiddos and colleagues? This is more important than a perfectly organized and executed lesson.

- Use words that will build up and encourage, not nag, complain, or tear down. If I want the culture of conversations in school to become healthier and more positive, it starts with me.

- Own the power God has placed on me. He's got me. Hold onto that.

- Live today showing unconditional love to those around me. For Christ has blessed me beyond measure by loving me unconditionally and by raining His grace upon my life.

- Rest in the loving and strong peace of God's arms. You are taken care of. Rest.

- Purposeful and intentional, prayerful planning.

- Actively pray for those around me. When someone is having a hard time or when I'm having a hard time being patient with them - pray.

- Write at least 3 thank you notes to students.

- Stay close to the Source. Rely on His strength.

- Be the light. Choose to be lighthearted today and have fun! When talking with colleagues, don't complain. Be a listener. Bring up funny points in the day.

- Take it a moment at a time and be thankful.

- Do one out-of-the-ordinary thing today that will bring me joy.

- Look up. When I am disheartened and looking down. When I am focused on myself and looking in. Even when I am distracted by everything around me and I look out, I will look up.

- Give myself the freedom to look at life with a fresh perspective.

- Slow down. Set the energy in the room. Pause to look around you. See what you notice. Be very present.

- Step up! Own your craft. Demonstrate the strengths and skills God has given me while being open and receptive to growth.

- Focus on your breathing.

GOING DEEPER
Memorable Moment Examples

Writing memories from the day is a practice I am developing. Whenever I write a memory, I am always incredibly grateful I did. Purposefully writing down the seemingly small, positive moments allows me to go back and revisit these times. I often return to these notes on the toughest days. When I feel weighed down by what feels like only heaviness and darkness, I can look to times when I saw light in my work and in my life. The memorable moments I write are often focused around these ideas:

- Meaningful conversations with students

- An unexpected positive moment

- A breakthrough moment while teaching a small group lesson

- A colleague who has helped me

- A lesson that went surprisingly well

- A special note or drawing I received

- A time when I saw students share their strengths or passions

- Moments when my students and I laughed together

- A funny or impactful quote I heard from a student

Notes

1. Yousafzai, Malala. Speaking to the United Nations General Assembly, 13 July 2013, New York.
2. Lewis, C.S. *The Abolition of Man*. Exciting Classics, 2013.
3. Aguilar, Elena. *Onward: Cultivating Emotional Resilience in Educators*. Jossey-Bass, 2018.
4. Montessori, Maria. *To Educate the Human Potential*. S.L., Aakar Books, 2019.
5. Stephens, Sydney. 2021. https://ssweetly.com.
6. Akṣapāda. *Living Toni Morrison: 425 Wise & Uplifting Verses of America's Beloved That You Should Read*. Independently published, 2019.
7. Covey, Stephen. *7 Habits of Highly Effective People*. Simon & Schuster Ltd, 2013.
8. Brown, Brené. *Dare to Lead: Brave Work, Tough Conversations, Whole Hearts*. Penguin Random House, 2018.
9. Crowther, Frank, and Andy Hargreaves. *Developing Teacher Leaders: How Teacher Leadership Enhances School Success*. Corwin Press, 2009.
10. Brown, Brené. *Rising Strong: How the Ability to Reset Transforms the Way We Live, Love, Parent, and Lead*. Penguin Random House, 2015.
11. Pierson, Rita. *Every Kid Needs a Champion*, TED Talks, 2013, https://www.youtube.com/watch?v=SFnMTHhKdkw.
12. Angelou, Maya. *Oprah Recalls One of Her Favorite Life Lessons from Maya Angelou*, OWN, 2011, https://youtu.be/BTiziwBhd54.
13. Tutu, Desmond and Mpho Tutu. *Book of Forgiving: The Fourfold Path for Healing Ourselves and Our World*. HarperCollins Publishers, 2015.
14. King, Martin Luther, Jr. *Strength to Love*. Collins-World, 1963.
15. Marais, Pepe. *Growing Greatness*. Jonathan Ball Publishers, 2018.
16. Brown, Brené. *Rising Strong: How the Ability to Reset Transforms the Way We Live, Love, Parent, and Lead*. Penguin Random House, 2015.
17. Nicholson, William, writer. *Shadowlands*. United International Pictures, 1993.
18. Pinkwater, Daniel Manus. *The Big Orange Splot*. Turtleback Books, 1993.
19. King, Martin Luther, Jr. *The Wisdom of Martin Luther King, Jr*. Plume Books, 1993.
20. Thnay, Vincent. *ABC of Quotes*. Lulu Press, Inc, 2015.
21. Speerstra, Karen. *The Green Devotional*. Mango Media, 2010.
22. "Our Dictionaries Oxford Languages." Oxford University Press, 2023, https://languages.oup.com/dictionaries/.
23. Lucado, Max. *Walking with the Savior*. Tyndale House Pub, 1993.
24. Chambers, Oswald. *My Utmost for His Highest*. Discovery House, 2018.
25. Adams, Henry. *Education of Henry Adams*. Blurb, 2019.
26. Burchard, Brendon. "The Brendon Show." *Brendon Burchard*. 2023. https://brendon.com/blog/.
27. O'Donohue, John. *To Bless the Space between Us: A Book of Blessings*. Doubleday, 2008.
28. Nichols, Morgan Harper. *https://www.instagram.com/morganharpernichols/*. 2019.
29. Ley, Emily. *Growing Boldly: Dare to Build a Life You Love*, Thomas Nelson, 2021.
30. King, Martin Luther, Jr. *Strength to Love*. 1963.
31. Young, Sarah. *Jesus Calling: Enjoying Peace in His Presence*. Thomas Nelson, 2019.

32. Beecher Stowe, Harriet. *Oldtown Folks*. Belknap Press, 2013.

33. Young, Sarah. *Jesus Today: Experience Hope Through His Presence*. Thomas Nelson, 2012.

34. Nouwen, Henri. *The Path of Waiting*. Crossroad Publishing Company, 1994.

35. Tutu, Desmond and Mpho Tutu. *Book of Forgiving: The Fourfold Path for Healing Ourselves and Our World*. HarperCollins Publishers, 2015.

36. Bond, Walter. "Pick Them Up Motivational Video Featuring Walter Bond," *YouTube*. 2019, https://youtu.be/rSsn2lru9rU.

37. Larson, Susie. *Blessings for the Morning*. Bethany House Publishers, 2014.

38. Nichols, Morgan Harper. *All Along You Were Blooming: Thoughts for Boundless Living*. Zondervan, 2020.

39. Kennedy, Kay, Lucy Leclerc, and Susan Campis. *Human-Centered Leadership in Healthcare: Evolution of a Revolution*. Morgan James Publishing, 2021.

40. Lucado, Max. *Grace for the Moment: Inspirational Thoughts for Each Day of the Year*. Thomas Nelson, 2013.

41. O'Donohue, John. *To Bless the Space between Us: A Book of Blessings*. Doubleday, 2008.

42. Brown, Brené. *Dare to Lead: Brave Work, Tough Conversations, Whole Hearts*. Penguin Random House, 2018.

43. Teresa, Mother. *A Call to Mercy: Hearts to Love, Hands to Serve*. Crown Publishing Group, 2016.

44. Tawwab, Nedra Glover. *Set Boundaries, Find Peace: A Guide to Reclaiming Yourself*. Penguin Publishing Group, 2021.

45. Esquith, Rafe. *Real Talk for Real Teachers: Advice for Teachers from Rookies to Veterans: "No Retreat, No Surrender!"* Penguin Books, 2014.

46. Chambers, Oswald. *My Utmost for His Highest*. Discovery House, 2018.

47. Oswald Chambers. *My Utmost for His Highest*. Discovery House, 2018.

48. Young, Sarah. *Jesus Today: Experience Hope Through His Presence*. Thomas Nelson, 2012.

49. Rohr, Richard. *Man's Approach to God*. St Anthony Messenger Pr., Audio cassette, 1987.

50. Brown, Brené. *The Gifts of Imperfection: Let Go of Who You Think You're Supposed to Be and Embrace Who You Are*. Hazelden, 2010.

51. Lucado, Max. *Grace for the Moment: Inspirational Thoughts for Each Day of the Year*. Thomas Nelson, 2013.

52. Cho, Eugene. "Vote to End Hunger - Bread for the World." *Exposure*, 2023, breadfortheworld.exposure.co/elections.

53. Nichols, Morgan Harper. *All Along You Were Blooming: Thoughts for Boundless Living*. Zondervan, 2020.

54. Hammond, Zaretta. *Culturally Responsive Teaching and the Brain: Promoting Authentic Engagement and Rigor among Culturally and Linguistically Diverse Students*. Corwin, 2015.

55. Obama, Michelle. *Becoming*. Penguin Books, 2018.

56. Adkins, Lucy, and Becky Breed. *Writing in Community*. BQB Publishing, 2013.

57. Frost, Robert. "The Road Not Taken," *Mountain Interval*. Henry Holt, 1916.

58. Beechick, Ruth. *An Easy Start in Arithmetic*. Mott Media, 1986.

59. Torrence, Antonio LaMar. *R.I.C.H. In Preaching*. Wipf and Stock Publishers, 2020.

60. Bartlett, Jayne. *Outstanding Assessment for Learning in the Classroom*. Routledge, 2015.
61. Esquith, Rafe. *Teach Like Your Hair's on Fire: The Methods and Madness Inside Room 56*. Viking, 2007.
62. Dweck, Carol. *Mindset: The New Psychology of Success*. Penguin Random House, 2006.
63. Williams, Leewin. *The Encyclopedia of Wit, Humor & Wisdom*. iUniverse, 2000.
64. Margerison, Charles. *Amazing Musicians*. Amazing People Club, 2012.
65. Katzer, Julius. *A.P. Chekhov 1860-1960*. Foreign Languages Publishing House, 1960.
66. Teresa, Mother. *A Call to Mercy: Hearts to Love, Hands to Serve*. Crown Publishing Group, 2016.
67. Hughes, Paul. *299 Quotations on Writing Creativity and Art*. Paul Hughes, 2012.
68. Hendricks, Bill, and Bev Hendricks Godby. *So How Do I Parent THIS Child?* Moody Publishers, 2021.
69. Poehler, Amy. *Yes Please*. Dey Street Books, 2015.
70. Tutu, Desmond and Mpho Tutu. *Book of Forgiving: The Fourfold Path for Healing Ourselves and Our World*. HarperCollins Publishers, 2015.
71. Thoreau, Henry David. *Walden or Life in the Woods*. Vintage Books, 1991.
72. Charbonneau, Bradley. *Spark: Ignite Initiative. We're Better Together*. Repossible, 2020.
73. Mckelvey, Douglas Kaine. *Every Moment Holy: New Liturgies for Daily Life*. Rabbit Room Press, 2017.
74. Duckworth, Angela. *Grit: Why Passion and Persistence Are the Secrets to Success*. Scribner, 2018.
75. Siegel, Seth. *Other People's Words*. St. Martin's Press, 2021.
76. McEntyre, Marilyn. *Christ, My Companion*. Wipf and Stock Publishers, 2012.
77. Colwell, Peter. *Invest in Your Attitude*. Jaico Publishing House, 2022.
78. Rohr, Richard. *Yes, And...: Daily Meditations*. Franciscan Media, 2019.
79. Teresa, Mother. *A Call to Mercy: Hearts to Love, Hands to Serve*. Crown Publishing Group, 2016.
80. Glasser, William. *The Quality School*. Harper Perennial, 1990.
81. Rowling, J.K. *Harry Potter and the Deathly Hallows*. Bloomsbury, 2007.
82. Angelou, Maya. *Maya Angelou 350+ Best Quotes*. The Source Publishing, 2014.
83. Lucado, Max. *Walking with the Savior*. Tyndale House, 1993.
84. Milne, A A, and Ernest H Shepard. *The House at Pooh Corner*. E.P. Dutton & Company, 2018.

(If there is a different source listed than the original author, as referenced in the text, the source listed is a secondary source which used the author's quote.)

ACKNOWLEDGEMENTS

For Teachers:

If I was your student, thank you for devoting your time, energy, and love into my life and this profession. You made an incredible impact on who I am today. I am a teacher because of you.

If I had the honor of teaching alongside you, thank you! You have inspired me to be a more loving, passionate person. You have supported me in my journey of becoming an educator. You have modeled how to advocate for students and love unconditionally. Thank you for your generosity toward myself and your students.

To My Circle:

Family and friends, there aren't words to express how deeply thankful I am for your love and encouragement. You have shown me unconditional support at every step of my journey. This book would not have been written without your inspiring belief, thoughtful perspectives, and unwavering prayers. I am so thankful to have such strong, passionate people in my life.

Thank You, God:

Heavenly Father, thank You for entrusting me with the task of writing this book. Thank You for putting a spark in my heart seven years ago to desire a text like this. While in the writing stages, there were so many moments when I felt overwhelmed and overjoyed by Your Holy Spirit's words. It has truly been a blessing to navigate this new experience. Thank You for calling me to the classroom and for strengthening me every step of the way.

About the Author

Cultivating Space

During my first year of teaching, I built a routine I cherish and continue to this day. When I leave for work, I always give myself an extra twenty minutes before I need to be in the classroom to prepare for the school day. After arriving at school, I sit in my car and share quiet time with God. I read Scripture and a meaningful devotional text, pray over my day, and set an intention for my time with students. This practice anchors my spiritual and professional life. When I have rushed mornings or early meetings and miss this sacred time, it evidences itself in my day. My attitude is less patient and grace-filled, and I am less grounded in my values.

My Bible, journal, devotional book, and a few bright pens always remain on the passenger seat of my car, waiting for the next morning. This sacred time is comforting and empowering to me. I can bring whatever is happening in my personal life to God and leave it in His care, trusting He will provide for all my needs that day. Then I "check it" at the car. I put on my school badge and leave my vehicle, ready (or not) for whatever adventures that day will hold.

The Inspiration Behind
"Called to the Classroom: Daily Reflections for Educators"

After I completed my undergraduate education, I was excited and nervous about beginning my new career as a teacher. I wanted to find a devotional resource specifically written with teachers in mind. I was hoping to discover a text combining the extravagant comfort and security of God's unconditional love with the incredible responsibility of the calling He had put before me. While I am sure there are many books like this, I struggled to find one that resonated with me. So, after six years of teaching, I decided to write one.

ABOUT THE AUTHOR (CONT.)

Background

Christina Meline graduated with her Bachelor of Science degree in Elementary Education and Bachelor of Arts degree in Biblical Studies from the University of Northwestern, St. Paul (Minnesota).

She completed her Master of Arts degree in Elementary Education from Winona State University (Minnesota).

Christina has taught in the classroom and online for over six years. She enjoys exploring new cities and states around the United States, meeting teachers and partnering with districts to empower educators.

Christina Meline is the founder of Team Meline, LLC, an organization dedicated to cultivating community and empowering educators. For more information about Christina and Team Meline visit: www.teammeline.com.

STAY CONNECTED
Uplift Educators Around You!

Interested in buying 10 or more copies?

For discounted bulk purchases of this book for your school, district, organization, or conference, please email me at christina.meline@teammeline.com

To book Christina Meline for interview or speaking events, visit www.teammeline.com/workshops/ or contact christina.meline@teammeline.com

For more daily reflections and additional resources, visit www.teammeline.com

Stay Connected!

I invite you to join our community to share your daily intentions, memorable moments, and authentic reflections.

Called to the Classroom

team.meline

www.teammeline.com

www.ingramcontent.com/pod-product-compliance
Lightning Source LLC
Chambersburg PA
CBHW021211130626
46554CB00004B/1172